THE CRUCIBLE

BY ARTHUR MILLER

DRAMATISTS
PLAY SERVICE
INC.

THE CRUCIBLE
Copyright © Renewed 1980, 1981, 1982, Arthur Miller
Copyright © 1952, 1953, 1954, Arthur Miller

All Rights Reserved

SPECIAL NOTE

THE CRUCIBLE was first presented by Kermit Bloomgarden at the Martin Beck Theatre, New York City, on January 22, 1953. It was directed by Jed Harris, and the scenery was designed by Boris Aronson. The cast was as follows:

BETTY PARRIS	Janet Alexander
REVEREND SAMUEL PARRIS	Fred Stewart
TITUBA	Jacqueline Andre
ABIGAIL WILLIAMS	Madeleine Sherwood
SUSANNA WALLCOTT	Barbara Stanton
MRS. ANN PUTNAM	Jane Hoffman
THOMAS PUTNAM	Raymond Bramley
MERCY LEWIS	Dorothy Jolliffe
MARY WARREN	Jenny Egan
JOHN PROCTOR	Arthur Kennedy
REBECCA NURSE	Jean Adair
GILES COREY	Joseph Sweeney
REVEREND JOHN HALE	E. G. Marshall
ELIZABETH PROCTOR	Beatrice Straight
FRANCIS NURSE	Graham Velsey
EZEKIEL CHEEVER	Don McHenry
JOHN WILLARD	George Mitchell
JUDGE HATHORNE	Philip Coolidge
DEPUTY-GOVERNOR DANFORTH	Walter Hampden
SARAH GOOD	Adele Fortin
HOPKINS	Donald Marye

SYNOPSIS OF SCENES

ACT I—SCENE 1: A bedroom in Reverend Samuel Parris' house, Salem, Massachusetts, in the spring of the year 1692.

ACT I—SCENE 2: The common room of Proctor's house, eight days later.

ACT II—SCENE 1: Five weeks later. A wood.

ACT II—SCENE 2: The vestry of the Salem Meeting House, two weeks later.

ACT II—SCENE 3: A cell in Salem jail, three months later.

The Play Service hereby acknowledges with grateful thanks the friendly help of Mr. Leonard Patrick, production stage manager of the Broadway production, for his aid in preparing this acting edition.

THE CRUCIBLE

ACT I

SCENE 1

A bedroom in Reverend Samuel Parris' house, Salem, Massachusetts, in the Spring of the year, 1692.

As the curtain rises we see Parris on his knees, beside a bed, situated in the C. of the stage. His daughter Betty, aged 10, is asleep in it, but the headboard blocks our view of her. The slow rising of light revealing the scene should imply the dawning of day. One emphatic source of light is at the L., but since the stage is surrounded by black velour freedom is given to light the area as the imagination requires. The only back drop in all scenes of the play is of black curtains at the back and sides of the stage. The curtains at the sides of the stage ("legs") are parallel to each other and parallel to the front of the stage. There are three of these curtains on each side of the stage. All entrances are made between these "legs." Across the back of the stage is one curtain. In front of the curtains is a misty bluish lighting effect. This can be achieved by a pipe of lights directly in front of the black back drop. Rays of light can extend slightly D. S. to be used as a definitive U. S. border for the acting area. This makes the black back drop less stark and produces a sheet of light to appear as the back wall of the set. The diagrams at the end of the text of this play show the arrangement of furniture as used in the Broadway production. Where entrances are shown, they are also located as they were in the Broadway production. Both entrances and furniture may be varied if the director wishes. In Act I—Scene 1 there is only one entrance from which all entrances and exits are made. This may be established wherever the director wishes. The mood must be one of high mystery, impending revelation. There will be a straight wooden chair to the Left of the bed, another at

5

R. and upstage of it, and a flat-topped clothes chest where convenient. The relative placing of these objects depends upon the acting scheme, rather than upon the requirements of the normal bedroom idea. In any case, the idea of this furniture is stark, utilitarian, and beautiful in that direct way. Across the back of the stage a curtain of bluish light relieves the blackness of the drapes. It will be possible for an actor to stand behind this light curtain, and to be barely visible to the audience as he awaits his entrance. Until he steps through this curtain he will be inactive, and in effect, not present in the scene. However, entrances may be made directly from offstage if preferred.

As Parris prays, Tituba appears behind the light curtain. She is his Negro slave, in her fifties. She hesitates before entering, then steps into the acting area, approaches her master, glancing over his back at the child on the bed.

TITUBA. My Betty be hearty soon?
PARRIS. Out of here!
TITUBA. My Betty not goin' die . . .
PARRIS. Out of my sight! Out of my . . . (Tituba exits hurriedly. He kneels again. He is overcome with sobs.) Oh, my God! God help me! (Quaking with a bodyful of fear, and uttering undecipherable syllables of sobs.) Betty. Child. Dear child. Will you wake, will you open up your eyes! Betty, little one . . . (Abigail Williams, 17, enters. A strikingly beautiful girl, an orphan, with an endless capacity for dissembling. Now she is all worry and apprehension and propriety.)
ABIGAIL. Uncle? Susanna Wallcott's here from Doctor Griggs.
PARRIS. Oh? The doctor. (Rising.) Let her come, let her come.
ABIGAIL. Come in, Susanna. (Susanna Wallcott, a little younger than Abigail, enters.)
PARRIS. What does the doctor say, child?
SUSANNA. Dr. Griggs he bid me come and tell you, Reverend sir, that he cannot discover no medicine for it in his books.
PARRIS. Then he must search on.
SUSANNA. Aye, sir, he have been searchin' his books since he left you, sir, but he bid me tell you, that you might look to unnatural things for the cause of it.

6

PARRIS. No—no. There be no unnatural causes here. Tell him I have sent for Reverend Hale of Beverly, and Mister Hale will surely confirm that. Let him look to medicine, and put out all thought of unnatural causes here. There be none.

SUSANNA. Aye, sir. He bid me tell you.

ABIGAIL. Speak nothin' of it in the village, Susanna.

PARRIS. Go directly home and speak nothin' of unnatural causes.

SUSANNA. Aye, sir. I pray for her. (Goes out.)

ABIGAIL. Uncle, the rumor of witchcraft is all about; I think you'd best go down and deny it yourself. The parlor's packed with people, sir.—I'll sit with her.

PARRIS. And what shall I say to them? That my daughter and my niece I discovered dancing like heathen in the forest?!

ABIGAIL. Uncle, we did dance; let you tell them I confessed it. But they're speakin' of witchcraft; Betty's not witched.

PARRIS. Abigail, I cannot go before the congregation when I know you have not opened with me. What did you do with her in the forest?

ABIGAIL. We did *dance*, Uncle, and when you leaped out of the bush so suddenly, Betty was frightened and then she fainted. And there's the whole of it.

PARRIS. Child. Sit you down.

ABIGAIL. I would never hurt Betty, I love her dearly, I . . .

PARRIS. Now look you, child—I have no desire to punish you; that will come in its time. But if you trafficked with spirits in the forest, I must know it, for surely my enemies will, and they'll ruin me with it. . . .

ABIGAIL. But we never conjured spirits.

PARRIS. Then why can she not move herself since midnight? This child is desperate! It must come out—my enemies will bring it out. Let me know what you done there. Abigail, do you understand that I have many enemies?

ABIGAIL. I know it, Uncle.

PARRIS. There is a faction that is sworn to drive me from my pulpit. Do you understand that?

ABIGAIL. I think so, sir.

PARRIS. Now then—in the midst of such disruption, my own household is discovered to be the very center of some obscene practice. Abominations are done in the forest. . . .

ABIGAIL. It were only sport, Uncle!

7

PARRIS. I saw Tituba waving her arms over the fire when I came on you; why were she doing that? And I heard a screeching and gibberish comin' from her mouth . . .

ABIGAIL. She always sings her Barbados songs, and we dance.

PARRIS. I cannot blink what I saw, Abigail—for my enemies will not blink it. I saw a dress lying in the grass.

ABIGAIL. A dress?

PARRIS. Aye, a dress. And I thought I saw a . . . someone naked running through the trees!

ABIGAIL. No one was naked! You mistake yourself, Uncle!

PARRIS. I saw it! Now tell me true, Abigail. Now my ministry's at stake; my ministry and perhaps your cousin's life. . . . Whatever abomination you have done, give me all of it now, for I dare not be taken unaware when I go before them down there.

ABIGAIL. There is nothin' more. I swear it, Uncle.

PARRIS. Abigail, I have fought here three long years to bend these stiff-necked people to me, and now, just now when there must be some good respect for me in the parish, you compromise my very character. I have given you a home, child, I have put clothes upon your back—now give me upright answer:—your name in the town—it is entirely white, is it not?

ABIGAIL. Why, I am sure it is, sir, there be no blush about my name.

PARRIS. Abigail, is there any other cause than you have told me, for Goody Proctor dischargin' you? It has troubled me that you are now seven months out of their house, and in all this time no other family has ever called for your service.

ABIGAIL. They want slaves, not such as I. Let them send to Barbados for that, I will not black my face for any of them! (*Enter Mrs. Ann Putnam. She is a twisted soul of forty-five, a death-ridden woman, haunted by dreams.*)

PARRIS. No—no, I cannot have anyone. Why, Goody Putnam, come in.

ANN. It is a marvel. It is surely a stroke of hell upon you. . . .

PARRIS. No, Goody Putnam, it is . . .

ANN. How high did she fly, how high?

PARRIS. No—no, she never flew. . . .

ANN. Why, it's sure she did; Mister Collins saw her goin' over Ingersoll's barn, and come down light as bird, he says!

PARRIS. Now, look you, Goody Putnam; she never . . . *Enter Thomas Putnam, a well-to-do, hard-handed landowner near fifty.*) Oh, good morning, Mister Putnam. . . .

PUTNAM. It is a providence the thing is out now! It is a providence.

PARRIS. What's out, sir, what's . . . ?

PUTNAM. (*Looking down at Betty.*) Why, her eyes is closed! Look you, Ann.

ANN. Why, that's strange. Ours is open.

PARRIS. Your little Ruth is sick?

ANN. I'd not call it *sick,* the Devil's touch is heavier than *sick,* it's *death,* y'know, it's death drivin' into them forked and hoofed.

PARRIS. Oh, pray not! Why, *how* does your child ail?

ANN. She ails as she must—she never waked this morning but her eyes open and she walks, and hears naught, sees naught, and cannot eat. Her soul is taken, surely.

PUTNAM. They say you've sent for Reverend Hale of Beverly?

PARRIS. A *precaution* only. He has much experience in all demonic arts, and I . . .

ANN. He has *indeed,* and found a *witch* in Beverly last year, and let you remember that.

PARRIS. Now, Goody Ann, they only thought that were a witch, and I am certain there be no element of witchcraft here.

PUTNAM. No witchcraft! Now look you, Mister Parris . . .

PARRIS. Thomas, Thomas, I pray you, *leap not to witchcraft.* I know that you, you least of all, Thomas, would ever wish so disastrous a charge laid upon me. We cannot leap to witchcraft. They will howl me out of Salem for such corruption in my house.

PUTNAM. Now, look you, Mister Parris; I have taken your part in all contention here, and I would continue; but I cannot if you hold back in this. There are hurtful, vengeful spirits layin' hands on these children.

PARRIS. But, Thomas, you cannot . . .

PUTNAM. Ann! Tell Mister Parris what you have done.

ANN. Reverend Parris, I have laid seven babies unbaptized in the earth. Believe me, sir, you never saw more hearty babies born. And yet, each would wither in my arms the very night of their birth. I have spoke nothin', but my heart has clamored intimations. And now, this year, my Ruth, my only—I see her turning strange. A secret child she has become this year, and shrivels like a sucking

9

mouth were pullin' on her life, too. And so I thought to send her
to your Tituba ——
PARRIS. To Tituba! What may Tituba . . . ?
ANN. Tituba knows how to speak to the *dead*, Mister Parris.
PARRIS. Goody Ann, it is a formidable sin to conjure up the dead!
ANN. I take it on my soul, (*Rising*.) but who else may surely tell
us what person murdered my babies.
PARRIS. Woman!
ANN. They were murdered, Mister Parris! And mark this *proof!*
—mark it! Last night my Ruth were ever so close to their little
spirits, I know it, sir. For how else is she struck dumb now except
some power of darkness would stop her mouth! It is a marvellous
sign, Mister Parris!
PUTNAM. Don't you understand it, sir? There is a murdering
witch among us bound to keep herself in the dark. Let your enemies make of it what they will, you cannot blink it more.
PARRIS. (*To Abigail*.) Then you were conjuring spirits last
night.
ABIGAIL. Not I, sir, not I.—Tituba and Ruth.
PARRIS. Now I am undone.
PUTNAM. You are not undone. Let you take hold here. Wait for
no one to charge you—declare it yourself. You have *discovered
witchcraft*. . . .
PARRIS. In my house!? In my house, Thomas?—they will topple
me with this! They will make of it a . . . (*Enter Mercy Lewis, a
sly, merciless girl of eighteen*.)
MERCY. Your pardons. . . . I only thought to see how Betty is.
PUTNAM. Why aren't you home? Who's with Ruth?
MERCY. Her grandma come. She's improved a little, I think—
she give a powerful sneeze before.
ANN. Ah, there's a sign of life!
MERCY. I'd fear no more, Goody Putnam, it were a grand sneeze;
another like it will shake her wits together, I'm sure.
PARRIS. Will you leave me now, Thomas, I would pray a while
alone. . . .
ABIGAIL. Uncle, you've prayed since midnight. Why do you not
go down and . . . ?
PARRIS. No—no. I'll wait till Mister Hale arrives.
PUTNAM. (*To Parris*.) Now *look* you, sir—let you strike out
against the Devil and the village will bless you for it! Come down,

speak to them—pray with them—they're thirsting for your word, Mister! Surely you'll pray with them.

PARRIS. I have no stomach for disputation this morning. I will lead them in a psalm. But let you say nothing of witchcraft yet. I will not discuss it. The cause is yet unknown. I have had enough contention since I came, I want no more. (*Putnam crosses* L. *to above table, gets hat, crosses and exits.*)

ANN. *Mercy*, you go home to Ruth, d'ye hear?

MERCY. Aye, Mum. (*Ann goes out.*)

PARRIS. If she starts for the window, cry for me at once. (*Crossing to door.*)

ABIGAIL. Yes, Uncle.

PARRIS. There is a terrible power in her arms today. (*Goes out with Putnam.*)

ABIGAIL. How is Ruth sick?

MERCY. It's weirdish, I know not—she seems to walk like a dead one since last night.

ABIGAIL. Betty? (*Betty doesn't move. She shakes her.*) Now stop this! Betty! Sit up now!

MERCY. Have you tried beatin' her? I gave Ruth a good one and it waked her for a minute. Here, let me have her. . . .

ABIGAIL. No, he'll be comin' up. Now look you, if they be questioning us tell them we danced—I told him as much already.

MERCY. And what more?

ABIGAIL. He saw you naked.

MERCY. Oh, Jesus! (*Falls back on bed. Enter Mary Warren, breathless. She is seventeen, a subservient, naive girl.*)

MARY. What'll we do, the whole village is out!

MERCY. (*Mimicking her.*) "What'll we do?" (*Sitting up.*)

MARY. I just come from the farm, the whole country's talkin' witchcraft! They'll be callin' us witches, Abby!

MERCY. (*Mimicking her.*) "They'll be callin' us witches, Abby." She means to tell, I know it.

MARY. Abby, we've got to tell. Witchery's a hangin' error, a hangin' like they done in Boston two year ago! We must tell the truth, Abby!—you'll only be whipped for dancin', and the other things!

ABIGAIL. Oh, *we'll* be whipped!

MARY. I never done none of it, Abby, I only looked!

MERCY. Oh, you're a great one for lookin', aren't you, Mary Warren?

11

ABIGAIL. (*Betty whimpers.*) Betty? Now, Betty, dear, wake up now. It's Abigail. (*She sits Betty up, furiously shakes her.*) I'll beat you, Betty! (*Betty whimpers.*) My, you seem improving. I talked to your papa and I told him everything. So there's nothing to . . .

BETTY. I want my mama!

ABIGAIL. What ails you, Betty? Your mama's dead and buried. . . .

BETTY. I'll fly to Mama, let me fly . . . ! (*Raises her arms as though to fly. Mercy and Abigail thrust them down.*)

ABIGAIL. I told him everything, he knows now, he knows everything we . . . (*Betty suddenly springs off bed, rushes across room to window where Abigail catches her.*)

BETTY. You drank blood, Abby, you drank blood!

ABIGAIL. (*Dragging Betty back to bed and forcing her into it.*) Betty, you never say that again! You will never . . .

BETTY. You did, you did! You drank a charm to kill John Proctor's wife! You drank a charm to kill Goody Proctor!

ABIGAIL. (*Slaps her face.*) Shut it! Now shut it!

BETTY. (*Collapsing on the bed.*) Mama, Mama . . . ! (*She dissolves into sobs.*)

ABIGAIL. Now look you. All of you. We danced. And Tituba conjured Ruth Putnam's dead sisters. And that is all. And mark this—let either of you breathe a word, or the edge of a word about the other things, and I will come to you in the black of some terrible night and I will bring a pointy reckoning that will shudder you. And you know I can do it; I saw Indians smash my dear parents' heads on the pillow next to mine, and I have seen some reddish work done at night, and I can make you wish you had never seen the sun go down! (*Betty cries louder. She goes to Betty, sits L. side of bed D. S. of Mercy, and roughly sits her up.*) Now you . . . sit up and stop this! (*Betty collapses in her hands.*)

MARY. What's got her? Abby, she's going to die! It's a sin to conjure and we . . .

ABIGAIL. I say shut it, Mary Warren! (*Enter John Proctor.*)

MARY. Oh! I'm just going home, Mister Proctor.

PROCTOR. Be you foolish, Mary Warren? Be you deaf? I forbid you leave the house, did I not? Why shall I pay you?—I am looking for you more often than my cows!

MARY. I only come to see the great doings in the world.

PROCTOR. I'll show you a great doin' on your arse one of these days. Now get you home; (*Mary crosses up and out.*) my wife is waitin' with your work!

MERCY. (*Rising, crossing to entrance. Titilated. Being aware of their relationship.*) I'd best be off. I have my Ruth to watch. . . . Good morning, Mister Proctor. (*Mercy sidles out. Since Proctor's entrance, Abigail has stood absorbing his presence, wide-eyed.*)

ABIGAIL. She's only gone silly, somehow. She'll come out of it.

PROCTOR. So she flies, eh? Where are her wings?

ABIGAIL. (*With a nervous laugh.*) Oh, John, sure you're not believin' she flies!

PROCTOR. The road past my house is a pilgrimage to Salem all morning. The town's mumbling witchcraft.

ABIGAIL. Oh, posh!—We were dancin' in the woods last night, and my uncle leaped in on us. She took fright, is all.

PROCTOR. (*His smile widens. Crossing to door.*) Dancin' by moonlight! (*Abigail springs into his path.*) You'll be clapped in the stocks before you're twenty.

ABIGAIL. (*Barring his way at door.*) Give me a word, John. A soft word.

PROCTOR. No—no, Abby, I've not come for that.

ABIGAIL. You come five mile to see a silly girl fly? I know you better.

PROCTOR. I come to see what mischief your uncle's brewin' now. Put it out of mind, Abby.

ABIGAIL. John—I am waitin' for you every night.

PROCTOR. Abby, you'll put it out of mind. I'll not be comin' for you more.

ABIGAIL. You're surely sportin' with me.

PROCTOR. You know me better.

ABIGAIL. I know how you clutched my back behind your house and sweated like a stallion whenever I come near! I saw your face when she put me out and you loved me then and you do now!

PROCTOR. Abby, that's a wild thing to say. . . .

ABIGAIL. A wild thing may say wild things. I have seen you since she put me out, I have seen you nights.

PROCTOR. I have hardly stepped off my farm this sevenmonth.

ABIGAIL. I have a sense for heat, John, and yours has drawn me to my window. Do you tell me you've never looked up at my window?

PROCTOR. Perhaps I . . . have.

ABIGAIL. I know you, John, I know you. (*She is weeping.*) I cannot sleep for dreamin', I cannot dream but I wake and walk about the house as though I'd find you comin' through some door.

PROCTOR. (*Taking her hands.*) Child . . .

ABIGAIL. (*With a flash of anger. Throwing his hands off.*) How do you call me child!

PROCTOR. (*As 3 or 4 persons off-stage begin a quiet chant—a psalm or hymn.*) Abby, I may think of you softly from time to time. But I will cut off my hand before I'll ever reach for you again. Wipe it out of mind—(*Takes her arms.*) we never touched, Abby.

ABIGAIL. (*Putting hands on his shoulders.*) Aye, but we did.

PROCTOR. (*Pushing her away.*) Aye, but we did not.

ABIGAIL. (*With a bitter anger.*) Oh, I marvel how such a (*Beating her fists against his chest.*) strong man may let such a sickly wife be . . .

PROCTOR. (*Coldly. Grabbing her wrists.*) You'll speak nothin' of Elizabeth!

ABIGAIL. She is blackening my name in the village! She is telling lies about me! She is a cold snivelling woman and you bend to her! Let her turn you like a . . . ?

PROCTOR. (*Shakes her.*) Do you look for whippin'!

ABIGAIL. (*Outraged. In tears.*) I look for John Proctor that put knowledge in my heart! I never knew what pretense Salem was, I never knew the lying lessons I was taught by all these Christian women and their covenanted men!—And now you bid me tear the light out of my eyes? I will not, I cannot! (*Shakes free.*) You loved me, John Proctor, and whatever sin it is you love me yet! (*He turns abruptly to go out. She rushes to door, blocks it.*) John, pity me, pity me! (*The words "Jehovah" are heard in the psalm —the song outside—Betty claps her ears suddenly, and whines loudly.*) Betty? (*She hurries to Betty, who is sitting up and screaming. Proctor crosses D. to U. L. of Abigail, who is trying to pull Betty's hands down, calling "Betty!" Proctor is growing unnerved, calling, "What's she doing? Girl, what ails you? Stop that wailin', Girl!" Singing has stopped in the midst of this, and Parris rushes in.*)

PARRIS. What happened? What are you doing to her! Betty! . . . (*Rushes to bed, crying "Betty, Betty!" As Ann crosses to*

14

*above Parris, feverish with curiosity, and with her Putnam, who
crosses to behind her.)*
ABIGAIL. She heard you singin' and suddenly she's up and
screamin' . . .
ANN. The psalm! The psalm!—she cannot bear to hear the Lord's
name!
PARRIS. No, God forbid. . . .
ANN. Mark it for a sign, mark it . . . ! *(Rebecca Nurse, 72, enters. She is white-haired, and leans upon her walking stick.)*
PUTNAM. That is a notorious sign of witchcraft afoot, a prodigious sign!
ANN. My mother told me that! When they cannot bear to hear
the name of . . .
PARRIS. Rebecca, Rebecca, come to her . . . we're lost, she sud-
denly cannot bear to hear the Lord's name. *(Rebecca crosses to
bed. Giles Corey enters. He is 83, knotted with muscle, canny,
inquisitive, and still powerful.)* There is hard sickness here, Giles
Corey, so please to keep the quiet.
COREY. I've not said a word. No one here can testify I've said a
word. Is she going to fly again? I hear she flies.
PUTNAM. Man, be quiet now! *(Rebecca stands by Betty, who be-
comes quiet.)*
ANN. What have you done?
REBECCA. Pray, calm yourselves. I have eleven children, and I
am twenty-six times a grandma, and I have seen them all through
their silly seasons, and when it come on them they will run the
Devil bowlegged keeping up with their mischief. I think she'll
wake when she tires of it. A child's spirit is like a child, you can
never catch it by running after it; you must stand still, and for
love it will soon itself come back.
PROCTOR. Aye, that's the truth of it, Rebecca.
ANN. This is no silly season, Rebecca. My Ruth is bewildered,
Rebecca, she cannot eat.
REBECCA. Perhaps she is not hungered yet. Mr. Parris, I hope
you are not decided to go in search of loose spirits. I've heard
promise of that outside. . . .
PARRIS. A wide opinion's running in the parish that the Devil
may be among us, and I would satisfy them that they are wrong.
PROCTOR. Then let you come out and call them wrong. Are you

15

our minister, or Mister Hale? Did you consult the wardens of the church before you called this minister to look for devils?

PARRIS. He is not coming to look for *devils!*

PROCTOR. Then what's he coming for?

PUTNAM. There be children dyin' in the village, Mister . . . !

PROCTOR. I see none dyin' . . .

REBECCA. Pray, John . . . be calm. Mister Parris, I think you'd best send Reverend Hale back as soon as he come. This will set us all to arguin' again in the society, and we thought to have peace this year. I think we ought rely on Doctor Griggs now, and good prayer. . . .

ANN. Rebecca, the doctor's baffled.

REBECCA. If so he is, then let us go to God for the cause of it. There is prodigious danger in the seeking of loose spirits, I fear it, I fear it. Let us rather blame ourselves and . . .

PUTNAM. How may we blame ourselves? I am one of nine sons; the Putnam seed have peopled this province. And yet I have but one child left of eight—and now she shrivels!

REBECCA. I cannot fathom that.

ANN. You think it God's work you should never lose a child, nor a grandchild either, and I bury all but one?

PUTNAM. When Reverend Hale comes you will proceed to look for signs of witchcraft here.

PROCTOR. You cannot command Mister Parris. We vote by name in this society, not by acreage.

PUTNAM. I never heard you worried so on this society, Mister Proctor. I do not think I saw you at Sabbath meeting since snow flew.

PROCTOR. I have trouble enough without I come five mile to hear him preach only hellfire and bloody damnation. There are many others who stay away from church these days because he hardly ever mention God any more.

PARRIS. Why, that's a drastic charge . . .

REBECCA. It's somewhat true; there are many that quail to bring their children . . .

PARRIS. I do not preach for children, Rebecca. It is not the *children* who are unmindful of their obligations toward this ministry. Where is my wood? My contract provides I be supplied with all my firewood. I am waiting since November for a stick, and even in November I had to show my frost-bitten hands like some London beggar!

COREY. You are allowed six pounds a year to buy your wood, Mister Parris.

PARRIS. I am paid little enough without I spend six pound on firewood. The salary is sixty-six pound, Mister Proctor! I am not some preaching farmer with a book under my arm; I am a graduate of Harvard College.

COREY. Aye, and well-instructed in mathematic!

PARRIS. Mister Corey, you will look far for a man of my kind at sixty pound a year! I am not *used* to this poverty; I left a thrifty business in the Barbados to serve the Lord. I do not fathom it, why am I persecuted here?! I cannot offer one proposition but there be a howling riot of argument. I have often wondered if the Devil be in it somewhere; I cannot understand you people otherwise.

PROCTOR. Mister Parris, you are the first minister ever did demand the deed to this house ——

PARRIS. I am your third preacher in seven years. I do not wish to be put out like the cat, whenever some majority feels the whim. You people seem not to comprehend that a minister is the Lord's man in the parish; a minister is not to be so lightly crossed and contradicted . . .

PUTNAM. Aye!

PARRIS. There is either obedience or the church will burn like hell is burning!

PROCTOR. Can you speak one minute without we land in hell again? I am sick of hell!

PARRIS. It is not for you to say what is good for you to hear!

PROCTOR. I may speak my heart, I think!

PARRIS. What, are we Quakers? We are not Quakers here yet, Mister Proctor. And you may tell that to your followers!

PROCTOR. My followers!

PARRIS. There is a *party* in this church; I am not blind; there is a faction and a party.

PROCTOR. Against *you?*

PUTNAM. Against him and all authority.

PROCTOR. Why, then I must find it and join it.

REBECCA. He does not mean that. . . .

PROCTOR. I mean it solemnly, Rebecca; I like not the smell of

17

this "authority," I have a crop to sow, and lumber to drag home. What say you, Giles? Let's find that party. He says there is a party.

COREY. I've changed my opinion of this man. Mister Parris, I beg your pardon. I never thought you had so much iron in you.

PARRIS. Why, thank you, Giles.

COREY. It suggest to the mind what the trouble be among us all these years. Think on it, wherefore is everybody suing everybody else. I have been six times in court this year.

PROCTOR. Is it the Devil's fault that a man cannot say you Good Morning without you clap him for defamation? You're old, Giles, and you're not hearing as well as you did.

COREY. John Proctor, I have only last month collected four pound damages for you publicly saying I burned the roof off your house, and I ——

PROCTOR. I never said no such thing, but I paid you for it, so I hope I can call you deaf without charge. Come along, Giles, and help me drag my lumber home.

COREY. I'll be damned first!

PUTNAM. A moment, Mister Proctor. What lumber is that you're draggin' home, if I may ask you?

PROCTOR. My lumber. From out my forest by the riverside.

PUTNAM. Why, we are surely gone wild this year: what anarchy is this?—that tract is in my bounds, it's in my bounds, Mister Proctor.

PROCTOR. In your bounds! I bought that tract from Goody Nurse's husband five months ago.

PUTNAM. He had no right to sell it. It stands clear in my grandfather's will that all the land between the river and . . .

PROCTOR. Your grandfather had a habit of willing land that never belonged to him, if I may say it plain.

COREY. That's God's truth; he nearly willed away my north pasture but he knew I'd break his fingers before he set his name to it. Let's get your lumber home, John, I feel a sudden will to work coming on.

PUTNAM. You load one oak of mine and you'll fight to drag it home!

COREY. Aye, and we'll win, too, Putnam—this fool and I. Come on!

PUTNAM. I'll have my men on you, Corey! I'll clap a writ on

you! (*Enter Reverend John Hale, 35, a ruddy, bright young man. He is loaded down with half a dozen heavy books.*)

HALE. Pray you, someone take these! (*Putnam crosses to Hale's L., helps him.*)

PARRIS. Mister Hale! Oh, it's good to see you again! (*Helping him as they cross D. to table.*) My, they're heavy!

HALE. (*Putting books on table.*) They must be, they are weighted with authority.

PARRIS. Well, you do come prepared!

HALE. We shall need hard study, if it comes to tracking down the Old Boy. You cannot be Rebecca Nurse?

REBECCA. I am, sir. Do you know me?

HALE. It's strange how I knew you, but I suppose you look as such a good soul should. We have all heard of your great charities in Beverly.

PARRIS. Do you know this gentleman?—Mister Thomas Putnam. And his good wife Ann.

HALE. Putnam! I had not expected such distinguished company, sir.

PUTNAM. It does not seem to help us today, Mister Hale. We look to you to come to our house and save our child.

HALE. Your child ails, too?!

ANN. Her soul, her soul seems flown away. She sleeps and yet she walks. . . .

PUTNAM. She cannot eat.

HALE. Cannot eat! (*To Proctor and Corey.*) Do you men *also* have afflicted children?

PARRIS. No, no, these are farmers. John Proctor . . .

COREY. He don't believe in witches.

PROCTOR. I never spoke on witches one way or the other. Will you come, Giles?

COREY. No—no, John, I think not. I have some few queer questions of my own to ask this fellow.

PROCTOR. I've heard you be a sensible man, Mister Hale—I hope you'll leave some of it in Salem. (*Proctor goes out.*)

PARRIS. Will you look at my daughter, sir? (*Hale crosses R. to bed, followed by Parris. Corey follows to U. L. of Parris. Leads Hale to the bed.*) She has tried to leap out the window; we discovered her this morning on the highroad, waving her arms as though she'd fly.

19

HALE. Tries to fly?

PUTNAM. She cannot bear to hear the Lord's name, Mister Hale; that's a sure sign of witchcraft afloat.

HALE. No—no. . . . Now let me instruct you. We cannot look to superstition in this. The Devil is precise; the marks of his presence are definite as stone and we must look only for his proper signs and judge nothing beforehand, and I must tell you all, that I shall not proceed unless you are prepared to believe me if I should find no trace of hell in this.

PARRIS. It is agreed, sir—it is agreed—we will abide by your judgment.

HALE. Good then. Now, sir, what were your first warning of this strangeness?

PARRIS. Why, sir . . . I discovered her . . . and my niece Abigail and ten or twelve of the other girls, dancing in the forest last night.

HALE. You permit dancing?!

PARRIS. No—no, it were secret. . . .

ANN. Mister Parris' slave has knowledge of conjurin', sir.

PARRIS. We cannot be sure of that, Goody Ann. . . .

ANN. I know it, sir. I sent my child . . . she should learn from Tituba who murdered her sisters.

REBECCA. Goody Ann! You sent a child to conjure up the dead . . . ?

ANN. (Hysterically.) Let God blame me, not you, not you, Rebecca! I'll not have you judging me any more! Mr. Hale, is it a natural work to lose seven children before they live a day?

PARRIS. Sssh!

HALE. (Leafing through the book.) Seven dead in childbirth?

ANN. Aye. (Hale looks in book.)

PARRIS. What book is that?

ANN. What's there, sir?

HALE. (With a tasty love of intellectual pursuit. Looking at open book.) Here is all the invisible world, caught, defined and calculated. (Now looking at them. They are all enthralled with this.) In these books the Devil stands stripped of all his brute disguises. Here are all your familiar spirits—your incubi and succubi, your witches that go by land, by air, and by sea; your wizards of the night and of the day. Have no fear now—we shall find him out if he has come among us, and I mean to crush him utterly if he

has shown his face! (*Corey crosses near bed, looking at Betty.*)
REBECCA. Will it hurt the child, sir?
HALE. I cannot tell. If she is truly in the Devil's grip we may have to rip and tear to get her free.
REBECCA. I think I'll go then. I am too old for this.
PARRIS. Why, Rebecca, we may open up the boil of all our troubles today!
REBECCA. Let us hope for that. (*Up toward door.*) I go to God for you, sir.
PARRIS. (*Opens door.*) I hope you do not mean we go to Satan here!
REBECCA. I wish I knew. (*She goes out.*)
PUTNAM. Come, Mister Hale, let's get on. Sit you here. (*Hale sits on stool.*)
COREY. Mister Hale . . . I have always wanted to ask a learned man—What signifies the readin' of strange books?
HALE. What books? (*Ann rises.*)
COREY. I cannot tell; she hides them.
HALE. Who does this?
COREY. Martha, my wife. I have waked at night many times and found her in a corner, readin' of a book. Now what do you make of that?
HALE. Why, that's not necessarily . . .
COREY. It discomfits me! Last night—mark this—I tried and tried and could not say my prayers. And then she close her book and walks out of the house, and suddenly—mark this—I could pray again!
HALE. Ah!—the stoppage of prayer—that is strange. (*Sits on bed, beside Betty.*) I'd like to speak further on that with you.
COREY. I'm not sayin' she's touched the Devil, now, but I'd admire to know *what* books she reads and *why* she hides them—she'll not answer me, y' see.
HALE. Aye, we'll discuss it. Now mark me, if the Devil is in her you will witness some frightful wonders in this room, so please to keep your wits about you. Mister Putnam, stand close in case she flies. (*Turns to Betty, helps her sit up.*) Now, Betty dear, will you sit up? (*Sits her up.*) H'mmmm. Can you hear me? I am John Hale, minister of Beverly. I have come to help you, dear. Do you remember my two little girls in Beverly?

21

PARRIS. How can it be the Devil? Why would he choose my house to strike?

HALE. What victory would the Devil have, to win a soul already had? It is the best the Devil wants, and who is better than the minister?

COREY. That's deep, Mister Parris, deep.

HALE. Does someone afflict you, child? It need not be a woman, mind you, or a man. Perhaps some bird, invisible to others, comes to you, perhaps a pig, or any beast at all. Is there some figure bids you fly? (*Pauses. Passes his hand over her face.*) In nomine Domini Sabaoth, sui filiique ite ad Infernos. (*Betty is laid back on pillow. Looks to Abigail.*) Abigail, (*Looks back to Betty.*) what sort of dancing were you doing with her in the forest?

ABIGAIL. Why—common dancing is all.

PARRIS. I think I ought to say that I—I saw a kettle in the grass where they were dancing.

ABIGAIL. That were only soup.

HALE. Soup? What sort of soup were in this kettle, Abigail?

ABIGAIL. Why, it were beans—and lintels, I think, and ——

HALE. Mister Parris, you did not notice, did you—any living thing in the kettle? A mouse, perhaps, a spider, a frog ——? (*Parris looks at her.*)

ABIGAIL. (*Hysterically, seeing Parris' look.*) That frog jumped in, we never put it in!

PARRIS. A frog, Abby!

ABIGAIL. We never put it in!

HALE. Abigail, it may be your cousin is dying —— Did you call the Devil last night?

ABIGAIL. I never called him! Tituba called him!

PARRIS. She called the Devil!

HALE. I should like to speak with Tituba.

PARRIS. (*Takes Ann to door, and returns as she goes out.*) Goody Ann, will you bring her up?

HALE. How did she call him?

ABIGAIL. I know not—she spoke Barbados.

HALE. Did you feel any strangeness when she called him? A sudden cold wind, perhaps? A trembling below the ground?

ABIGAIL. I didn't see no Devil!—(*To Betty, frantically.*) Betty, wake up, Betty! Betty!

HALE. You cannot evade me, Abigail.—Did your cousin drink any of the brew in that kettle?

ABIGAIL. She never drank it!

HALE. Did you drink it?

ABIGAIL. No, sir!

HALE. Did Tituba ask you to drink it?

ABIGAIL. She tried but I refused.

HALE. *Why* are you concealing? Have you sold yourself to Lucifer?

ABIGAIL. I never sold myself! I'm a good girl—I—(*Ann enters with Tituba.*) I did drink of the kettle!—She made me do it! She made Betty do it!

TITUBA. Abby!

ABIGAIL. She makes me drink blood!

PARRIS. Blood!!

ANN. My baby's blood?

TITUBA. No—no, chicken blood, I give she chicken blood!

HALE. Woman, have you enlisted these children for the Devil?

TITUBA. No—no, sir, I don't truck with the Devil!

HALE. (*Of Betty.*) Why can she not wake? Are you silencing this child?

TITUBA. I love me Betty!

HALE. You have sent your spirit out upon this child, have you not? Are you gathering souls for the Devil?

ABIGAIL. She send her spirit on me in *church,* she make me laugh at *prayer!*

PARRIS. She have often laughed at prayer!

ABIGAIL. She comes to me every night to go and drink blood!

TITUBA. You beg *me* to conjure, Abby! She beg *me* make charm ——

ABIGAIL. I'll tell you something. She comes to me while I sleep; she's always making me dream corruptions!

TITUBA. Abby!

ABIGAIL. (*At* R. *of Betty's head. Hysterically, horrified.*) Sometimes I wake and find myself standing in the open doorway and not a stitch on my body! (*Covering herself with her arms, turning up stage and away.*) I always hear her laughing in my sleep. I hear her singing her Barbados songs and tempting me with ——

TITUBA. Mister Reverend, I never —— } (*Together.*)

HALE. Tituba, I want you to wake this child. }

23

TITUBA. I have no power on this child, sir.

HALE. You most certainly do, and you will loose her from it now! When did you compact with the Devil?

TITUBA. I don't compact with no Devil!

PARRIS. You will confess yourself or I will take you out and whip you to your death, Tituba!

PUTNAM. This woman must be hanged! She must be taken and hanged!

TITUBA. (*Kneeling.*) No—no, don't hang Tituba. I tell him I don't desire to work for him, sir.

HALE. Who, the Devil? Now, Tituba, I know that when we bind ourselves to Hell it is very hard to break with it entirely. Now, we are going to help you tear yourself free.—You would be a good Christian woman, would you not, Tituba?

TITUBA. Ay, sir, a good Christian woman.

HALE. And you love these little children?

TITUBA. Oh, yes, sir, I don't desire to hurt little children?

HALE. And you love God, Tituba?

TITUBA. I love God with all my bein'.

HALE. Now in God's holy name . . .

TITUBA. Bless Him . . . bless Him. . . .

HALE. And to His Glory . . .

TITUBA. Eternal Glory. . . . Bless Him. . . . Bless God. . . .

HALE. Open yourself, Tituba—open yourself and let God's holy light shine on you.

TITUBA. Oh, bless the Lord.

HALE. When the devil comes to you does he ever come . . . with another person? Perhaps another person in the village? Someone you know.

PARRIS. Who came with him?

PUTNAM. Sarah Good? Did you ever see Sarah Good with him? —or Osborn?

PARRIS. Was it man or woman came with him?

TITUBA. Was . . . was woman.

PARRIS. What woman? A woman, you said. What woman?

TITUBA. It was black dark, and I . . .

PARRIS. You could see him, why could you not see her?

TITUBA. Well, they was always talking, they was always runnin' round and carryin' on.

PARRIS. You mean out of Salem? Salem witches? (*Hale indicates to Parris to take it easy.*)

TITUBA. I believe so, yes, sir.

HALE. (*Calmly. Now he takes her hand.*) Tituba. You must have no fear to tell us who they are, do you understand? We will protect you. The Devil can never overcome a minister. You know that, do you not?

TITUBA. Aye, sir, oh, I *do.*

HALE. You have confessed yourself to witchcraft, and that speaks a wish to come to heaven's side. And we will bless you, Tituba. . . .

TITUBA. (*Deeply relieved.*) Oh, God bless you, Mister Hale . . . !

HALE. You are God's *instrument* put in our hands to discover the Devil's agents among us. You are selected, Tituba, you are chosen to help us cleanse our village. So speak utterly, Tituba, turn your back on him and face God, face God, Tituba, and God will protect you.

TITUBA. Oh, God, protect Tituba!

HALE. Who came to you with the Devil? Two? Three? Four?—how many?

TITUBA. (*She pants, and begins rocking back and forth, staring ahead.*) There was four. There was four.

PARRIS. Who? Who? Their names, their names!

TITUBA. Oh, how many times he bid me kill you, Mister Parris!

PARRIS. Kill me!

TITUBA. (*Starting to weep.*) He say Mister Parris must be kill! Mister Parris no goodly man, Mister Parris mean man and no gentle man, and he bid me rise out of my bed and cut your throat! (*Parris backs away a step L., then all straighten up. They gasp.*) I tell him, no! I don't hate that man! I don't want kill that man! But he say, You work for me, Tituba, and I make you free! I give you pretty dress to wear, and put you way high up in the air and you gone fly back to Barbados! And I say, You lie, Devil, you lie! And then he come one stormy night to me, and he say, Look! I have white people belong to me. And I look. . . . And there was Goody Good.

PARRIS. Sarah Good!

TITUBA. (*Rocking violently.*) Aye, sir, and Goody Osburn. . . .

ANN. I knew it! Goody Osburn were midwife to me three times.

25

I begged you, Thomas, did I not? I begged him not to call Osburn because I feared her, my babies always shrivelled in her hands. . . .

HALE. (*During this Tituba is crying praises to the Lord.*) Take courage, you must give us all their names. How can you bear to see these children suffering? Look at them, Tituba—(*He is indicating Betty on the bed.*) look at their God-given innocence; their souls are so tender; we must protect them, Tituba; the Devil is out and preying on them like a beast upon the flesh of the pure lamb. . . . God will bless you for your help. . . .

ABIGAIL. (*Hands clasped, eyes closed.*) I want to open myself! I want the light of God, I want the sweet love of Jesus! I danced for the Devil; I saw him; I wrote in his book; I go back to Jesus; I kiss His hand—I saw Sarah Good (*Betty's hands appear above headboard raised toward heaven.*) with the Devil! I saw Goody Osburn with the devil! I saw Bridget Bishop with the Devil! (*As she is speaking Betty picks it up as a chant.*)

BETTY. (*As all turn to her.*) I saw George Jacobs with the Devil! I saw Goody Howe with the Devil!

PARRIS. She speaks. She speaks!

HALE. Glory to God!—it is broken, they are free!

BETTY. (*Calling it out hysterically and with great relief.*) I saw Martha Bellows with the Devil!

ABIGAIL. (*It is rising to a great glee.*) I saw Goody Sibber with the Devil!

PUTNAM. The marshal, I'll call the marshal!

HALE. Let the marshal bring irons.

BETTY. I saw Alice Barrow with the Devil!

BETTY. I saw Goody Pike with the Devil. ⎫
ABIGAIL. I saw Goody Hawkins with the ⎬ (*Together.*)
Devil . . . ! ⎭

ABIGAIL. I saw Mister Barton with the Devil!

BETTY. I saw Goody Cobb with the Devil.

ABIGAIL. I saw Goody Franklin with the Devil.

BETTY. I saw Goody Hopper with the Devil. (*On their ecstatic cries, CURTAIN FALLS.*)

ACT I

SCENE 2

Proctor's house, eight days later. Arrangement of furniture is indicated in diagram. On back of wash stand D. R. *is a nail on which hangs Elizabeth's shawl. On* U. S. *end of bench at* R. C. *is a nail to support gun which Proctor leans against bench. In the same bench is a hole in which is a whip. There are two entrances, one to outside of house,* D. L., *the other leading to rest of house, either* D. R. *or* U. R.

On the rise, the common room is empty. From above Elizabeth is heard softly singing to the children. John Proctor enters D. R., *carrying his gun, three seconds after curtain. He glances about the room. Crosses to wall* U. C., *leans gun against bench* R. *Crosses* D. R. *to wash stand, pours water into it from pitcher. As he is washing, Elizabeth's footsteps are heard. Elizabeth enters,* D. L.

ELIZABETH. What keeps you so late? It's almost dark.

PROCTOR. I were planting far out to the forest edge.

ELIZABETH. Oh, you're done then.

PROCTOR. Aye, the farm is seeded. The boys asleep? (*Dips hands in water, wipes them.*)

ELIZABETH. (*Removes water and towel, goes out* L., *and returns with dish of stew.*) They will be soon. (*Serves stew in a dish.*)

PROCTOR. Pray now for a fair summer.

ELIZABETH. (*Goes out* L., *returns with another dish.*) Aye.

PROCTOR. Are you well today?

ELIZABETH. I am. It is a rabbit.

PROCTOR. Oh, is it! In Jonathan's trap?

ELIZABETH. No, she walked into the house this afternoon; I found her sittin' in the corner like she come to visit.

PROCTOR. Oh, that's a good sign walkin' in.

ELIZABETH. Pray God. It hurt my heart to strip her, poor rabbit.

PROCTOR. Oh, it is well seasoned.

ELIZABETH. I took great care. She's tender?

27

PROCTOR. Aye. I think we'll see green fields soon. It's warm as blood beneath the clods.

ELIZABETH. That's well.

PROCTOR. If the crop is good I'll buy George Jacobs' heifer. How would that please you?

ELIZABETH. Aye, it would.

PROCTOR. I mean to please you, Elizabeth.

ELIZABETH. (*It is hard to say.*) I know it, John.

PROCTOR. (*As gently as he can.*) Cider?

ELIZABETH. (*A sense of her reprimanding herself for having forgot.*) Aye! (*Gets jug from off* L., *pours drink into pewter mug, brings it to him.*)

PROCTOR. This farm's a continent when you go foot by foot droppin' seeds in it.

ELIZABETH. It must be.

PROCTOR. On Sunday let you come with me and we'll walk the farm together; I never see such a load of flowers on the earth. Massachusetts is a beauty in the spring!

ELIZABETH. Aye, it is.

PROCTOR. I think you're sad again. Are you?

ELIZABETH. You come so late I thought you'd gone to Salem this afternoon.

PROCTOR. Why? I have no business in Salem.

ELIZABETH. You did speak of goin', earlier this week.

PROCTOR. I thought better of it, since.

ELIZABETH. Mary Warren's there today.

PROCTOR. Why'd you let her? You heard me forbid her go to Salem any more!

ELIZABETH. I couldn't stop her.

PROCTOR. It is a fault, it is a fault, Elizabeth—you're the mistress here, not Mary Warren.

ELIZABETH. She frightened all my strength away. . . .

PROCTOR. How may that mouse frighten you, Elizabeth? You . . .

ELIZABETH. It is no mouse no *more*. I forbid her go, and she raises up her chin like the daughter of a prince, and says to me, "I must go to Salem, Goody Proctor, I am an official of the court!"

PROCTOR. Court! What court?

ELIZABETH. Ay, it is a proper court they have now. They've sent four judges out of Boston, she says, weighty magistrates of the General Court, and at the head sits the Deputy Governor of the Province.

PROCTOR. (*Astonished.*) Why, she's mad.

ELIZABETH. I would to God she were. There be fourteen people in the jail now, she says. And they'll be tried, and the court have power to hang them too, she says.

PROCTOR. Ah, they'd never hang. . . .

ELIZABETH. The Deputy Governor promise hangin' if they'll not confess, John. The town's gone wild, I think—Mary Warren speak of Abigail as though she were a saint, to hear her. She brings the other girls into the court, and where she walks the crowd will part like the sea for Israel. And folks are brought before them, and if Abigail scream and howl and fall to the floor— the person's clapped in the jail for bewitchin' her. (*He can't look at her.*)

PROCTOR. Oh, it is a black mischief.

ELIZABETH. I think you must go to Salem, John. I think so. You must tell them it is a fraud.

PROCTOR. Aye, it is, it is surely.

ELIZABETH. Let you go to Ezekiel Cheever—he knows you well. And tell him what she said to you last week in her uncle's house. She said it had naught to do with witchcraft, did she not?

PROCTOR. (*In thought. Sighing.*) Aye, she did, she did.

ELIZABETH. (*Quietly, fearing to anger him by prodding. A step L.*) God forbid you keep that from the court, John; I think they must be told.

PROCTOR. Ay, they must, they must. . . . It is a wonder that they do believe her.

ELIZABETH. I would go to Salem now, John . . . let you go tonight.

PROCTOR. I'll think on it.

ELIZABETH. (*With her courage now.*) You cannot keep it, John.

PROCTOR. (*Angering.*) I know I cannot keep it. I say I will think on it!

ELIZABETH. (*Hurt, and very coldly.*) Good then, let you think on it.

PROCTOR. (*Defensively.*) I am only wondering how I may prove what she told me, Elizabeth. If the girl's a saint now, I think it is not easy to prove she's fraud, and the town gone so silly. She told it to me in a room alone—I have no proof for it.

29

ELIZABETH. You were alone with her?

PROCTOR. For a moment alone, aye.

ELIZABETH. Why, then, it is not as you told me.

PROCTOR. For a moment, I say. The others come in soon after.

ELIZABETH. Do as you wish, then.

PROCTOR. Woman. I'll not have your suspicion any more.

ELIZABETH. (*A little loftily.*) I have no . . .

PROCTOR. I'll not have it!

ELIZABETH. Then let you not earn it.

PROCTOR. (*With a violent undertone.*) You doubt me yet?!

ELIZABETH. John, if it were not Abigail that you must go to hurt, would you falter now? I think not.

PROCTOR. Now look you . . .

ELIZABETH. I see what I see, John.

PROCTOR. You will not judge me more, Elizabeth. I have good reason to think before I charge fraud on Abigail, and I will think on it. Let you look to your own improvement before you go to judge your husband any more. I have forgot Abigail, and . . .

ELIZABETH. And I.

PROCTOR. Spare me! You forget nothing and forgive nothing. Learn charity, woman. I have gone tiptoe in this house all seven-month since she is gone; I have not moved from there to there without I think to please you, and still a . . . an everlasting funeral marches round your heart. I cannot speak but I am doubted; every moment judged for lies as though I come into a court when I come into this house!

ELIZABETH. (*Firmly.*) John, you are not open with me. You saw her with a crowd, you said. Now, you . . .

PROCTOR. I'll plead my honesty no more, Elizabeth.

ELIZABETH. (*Now she would justify herself.*) John, I am only . . .

PROCTOR. (*In outburst.*) No more! I should have roared you down when first you told me your suspicion. But I wilted, and like a Christian, I confessed. Some dream I had must have mistaken you for God that day, but you're not, you're not. Let you remember it. Let you look sometimes for the goodness in me, and judge me not.

ELIZABETH. I do not judge you. The magistrate sits in your heart that judges you. I never thought you but a good man, John, only somewhat bewildered.

PROCTOR. Oh, Elizabeth, your justice would freeze beer. (*He turns suddenly toward a sound outside. Mary Warren enters R.*) How do you go to Salem when I forbid it! Do you mock me? I'll whip you if you dare leave this house again!

MARY. (*Weakly, sickly.*) I am sick, I am sick, Mister Proctor. Pray, pray, hurt me not. My insides are all shuddery; I am in the proceedings all day, sir.

PROCTOR. (*Angrily in a loud voice as Mary is crossing.*) And what of these proceedings here?—when will you proceed to keep this house as you are paid *nine pound* a year to do?—and my wife not wholly well?

MARY. (*Crossing L. to Elizabeth, taking small rag doll from pocket in her undershirt.*) I made a gift for you today, Goody Proctor. I had to sit long hours in a chair, and passed the time with sewing.

ELIZABETH. (*Perplexed, she looks at the doll.*) Why, thank you, it's a fair poppet.

MARY. (*Fervently, with a trembling, decayed voice.*) We must all love each other now, Goody Proctor.

ELIZABETH. (*Amazed at her strangeness.*) —Aye, indeed we must.

MARY. I'll get up early in the morning and clean the house. I must sleep now.

PROCTOR. Mary. Is it true there be fourteen women arrested?

MARY. No, sir. There be thirty-nine now. . . . (*She suddenly breaks off and sobs.*)

ELIZABETH. (*Rising and crossing to Mary.*) Why, she's weepin'! What ails you, child?

MARY. Goody Osburn . . . will hang! (*Elizabeth hugs her.*)

PROCTOR. Hang! Hang, y'say?

MARY. Aye. . . .

PROCTOR. The Deputy Governor will permit it?

MARY. If sentenced her. Hu must   (*Taking her head from Elizabeth's shoulder. To ameliorate it.*) But not Sarah Good. For Sarah Good confessed, y'see.

PROCTOR. Confessed! To what?

MARY. That she sometimes made a compact with Lucifer, and wrote her name in his black book—with her blood—and bound herself to torment Christians till God's thrown down . . . and we all must worship Hell forevermore. (*Elizabeth puts doll on table.*)

31

PROCTOR. But . . . surely you know what a jabberer she is. Did you tell them that?

MARY. Mister Proctor, in open court she near to choked us all to death.

PROCTOR. *How* choked you?

MARY. She sent her *spirit* out.

ELIZABETH. Oh, Mary, Mary, surely you . . .

MARY. She tried to kill me many times, Goody Proctor!

ELIZABETH. Why, I never heard you mention that before.

MARY. (*Innocently.*) I never *knew* it before. I never knew anything before. When she come into the court I say to myself, I must not accuse this woman, for she sleep in ditches, and so very old and poor. . . . But then . . . then she sit there, denying and denying, and I feel a misty coldness climbin' up my back, and the skin on my skull begin to creep, and I feel a clamp around my neck and I cannot breathe air; and then . . . (*Entranced as though it were a miracle.*) I hear a voice, a screamin' voice, and it were *my* voice . . . and all at once I remembered everything she done to me! (*Slight pause as Proctor watches Elizabeth pass him, then speaks, being aware of Elizabeth's alarm.*)

PROCTOR. (*Looking at Elizabeth.*) Why?—What did she do to you?

MARY. (*Like one awakened to a marvelous secret insight.*) So many time, Mister Proctor, she come to this very door beggin' bread and a cup of cider—and mark *this*—whenever I turned her away empty—she *mumbled.*

ELIZABETH. Mumbled! She may mumble, hungry.

MARY. But *what* does she mumble? You must remember, Goody Proctor—last month—a Monday, I think—she walked away and I thought my *guts* would burst for two days after. Do you remember it?

ELIZABETH. Why . . . I do, I think, but . . .

MARY. And so I told that to Judge Hathorne, and he asks her so —"Goody Good," says he, "what *curse* do you mumble that this girl must fall sick after turning you away?" And then she replies: (*Mimicking an old crone.*) —"Why, your excellence, no curse at all; I only say my commandments; I hope I may say my commandments," says she!

ELIZABETH. And that's an upright answer.

MARY. Aye, but then Judge Hathorne say, "Recite for us your

commandments!"—and of all the ten she could not say a single
one. She never knew no commandments, and they had her in a
flat lie!

PROCTOR. And so condemned her?

MARY. (*Impatient at his stupidity.*) Why, they *must* when she
condemned herself.

PROCTOR. But the proof, the proof?

MARY. (*With greater impatience with him.*) I *told* you the proof
—it's hard proof, hard as rock the judges said.

PROCTOR. You will not go to that court again, Mary Warren.

MARY. (*Defiantly.*) I must tell you, sir, I will be gone *every day*
now. I am *amazed* you do not see what weighty work we do.

PROCTOR. What work you do! It's strange work for a Christian
girl to hang old women!

MARY. But, Mister Proctor, they will not *hang* them if they
confess. Sarah Good will only sit in *jail* some time . . . and here's
a *wonder* for you, think on this. Goody Good is pregnant!

ELIZABETH. Pregnant! Are they mad?—the woman's near to
sixty!

MARY. (*Happy with wonders of the court.*) They had Doctor
Griggs examine her and she's full to the brim. And smokin' a
pipe all these years and no *husband either!*—but she's safe, thank
God; for they'll not hurt the innocent *child.* (*Smiling happily.*) But
be that not a *marvel?* You *must* see it, sir, it's God's work we do.
. . . So I'll be gone every day for some time. I'm . . . I am an
official of the court, they say, and I . . .

PROCTOR. I'll official you! (*Rises, gets whip.*)

MARY. (*Striving for her authority.*) I'll not stand *whipping any
more!* The Devil's loose in Salem, Mister Proctor, we must discover where he's hiding!

PROCTOR. I'll whip the Devil out of you . . . ! (*With whip
raised she yells.*)

MARY. (*Pointing at Elizabeth.*) I *saved* her life today! (*Silence.
His whip comes down.*)

ELIZABETH. (*Softly.*) I am accused?

MARY. You are somewhat mentioned. But I said I never see no
sign you ever sent your spirit out to hurt no one, and seeing I do
live so closely with you, they dismissed it.

ELIZABETH. Who accused me?

MARY. I am bound by law; I cannot tell it. (*To Proctor.*) I . . .

33

I hope you'll not be so sarcastical no more—four judges and the King's deputy sat to dinner with us but an hour ago. I . . . I would have you speak civilly to me, from this out.

PROCTOR. (*In disgust at her.*) Go to bed.

MARY. I'll not be ordered to bed *no more*, Mister Proctor! I am eighteen and a woman, however single!

PROCTOR. Do you wish to sit up?—then sit up.

MARY. (*Stamping foot.*) I wish to go to bed!

PROCTOR. (*In anger.*) Good night, then! (*She starts out L.*)

MARY. Good night. (*She goes out L. He throws whip down.*)

ELIZABETH. Oh, the noose, the noose is up!

PROCTOR. There'll be no noose. . . .

ELIZABETH. She wants me dead; I knew all week it would come to this!

PROCTOR. (*Without conviction.*) They dismissed it. You heard her say . . .

ELIZABETH. And what of tomorrow?—she will cry me out until they take me!

PROCTOR. Sit you down. . . .

ELIZABETH. She wants me dead, John, you know it!

PROCTOR. I say sit down! Now we must be wise, Elizabeth.

ELIZABETH. (*With sarcasm, and a sense of being lost.*) Oh, indeed, indeed!

PROCTOR. (*Not looking at her.*) Fear nothing. I'll find Ezekiel Cheever. I'll tell him she said it were all sport.

ELIZABETH. John, with so many in the jail, more than that is needed now, I think. Would you favor me with this?—Go to *Abigail*.

PROCTOR. What have I to say to Abigail?

ELIZABETH. John . . . grant me this. You have a faulty understanding of young girls. There is a promise made in any bed . . .

PROCTOR. (*Striving against his anger. Looking at her.*) What promise?

ELIZABETH. Spoke or silent, a promise is surely made. And she may dote on it now—I am sure she does—and thinks to kill me, then to take my place. It is her dearest hope, John, I know it. There be a thousand names, why does she call mine? There be a certain danger in calling such a name—I am no Goody Good that sleeps in ditches, nor Osburn drunk and half-witted. She'd

34

dare not call out such a farmer's wife but there be monstrous profit in it. She thinks to take my place, John.

PROCTOR. (*He knows it is true.*) She cannot think it!

ELIZABETH. John, have you ever shown her somewhat of contempt? She cannot pass you in the church but you will blush . . .

PROCTOR. I may blush for my sin.

ELIZABETH. I think she sees another meaning in that blush.

PROCTOR. And what see you? What see you, Elizabeth?

ELIZABETH. I think you be somewhat ashamed, for I am there, and she so close.

PROCTOR. When will you know me, woman? Were I stone I would have cracked for shame this seven-month!

ELIZABETH. Then go—and tell her she's a whore. Whatever promise she may sense—break it, John, break it.

PROCTOR. (*Rising, getting gun.*) Good, then. I'll go.

ELIZABETH. Oh, how unwillingly!

PROCTOR. I will curse her hotter than the oldest cinder in hell, fear not. But pray, begrudge me not my anger!

ELIZABETH. Your anger! I only ask you . . .

PROCTOR. Woman, am I so base? Do you truly think me base?

ELIZABETH. I never called you base.

PROCTOR. Then how do you charge me with such a promise! The promise that a stallion gives a mare I gave that girl!

ELIZABETH. Then why do you anger with me when I bid you break it?

PROCTOR. (*So angry he gropes for words and phrases.*) Because it speaks deceit, and I am honest! But I'll plead no more! I see now your spirit twists around the single error of my life, and I will never tear it free!

ELIZABETH. (*Cries out.*) You'll tear it free—when you come to know that I will be your only wife, or no wife at all!—she has an arrow in you yet, John Proctor, and you know it well! (*Proctor starts it. Quite suddenly as though from the air, Hale appears n. They start slightly. Hale is different now, drawn—a little, even, of guilt about his manner now.*)

HALE. Good evening.

PROCTOR. Why, Mister Hale! Good evening to you, sir. Come in, come in.

HALE. I hope I do not startle you.

ELIZABETH. No—no, it's only that I heard no horse. . . .

35

HALE. You are Goodwife Proctor.

PROCTOR. Aye: Elizabeth.

HALE. I hope you're not off to bed yet.

PROCTOR. No—no . . . let you come in, Mister Hale. We are not used to visitors after dark, but you're welcome here. Will you sit you down, sir?

HALE. I will. Let you sit, Goodwife Proctor.

PROCTOR. Will you drink cider, Mister Hale?

HALE. No, it rebels my stomach—I have some further travelling yet tonight. Sit you down, sir. I will not keep you long, but I have some business with you.

PROCTOR. Business of the court?

HALE. (*Hesitantly.*) No . . . no, I come of my own, without the court's authority. Hear me. I know not if you are aware, but your wife's name is . . . mentioned in the court.

PROCTOR. We know it, sir. Our Mary Warren told us. We are entirely amazed.

HALE. I am a stranger here, as you know. And in my ignorance, I find it hard to draw a clear opinion of them that come accused before the court. And so this afternoon, and now tonight, I go from house to house. . . . I come now from Rebecca Nurse's house and . . .

ELIZABETH. (*Shocked.*) Rebecca's charged!

HALE. God forbid such a one be charged. She is, however . . . mentioned somewhat.

ELIZABETH. You will never believe, I hope, that Rebecca trafficked with the Devil?

HALE. (*Regretfully.*) Woman, it is possible.

PROCTOR. (*Taken aback.*) Surely you cannot think so.

HALE. This is a strange time, Mister. No man may longer doubt the powers of the dark are gathered in monstrous attack upon this village. There is too much evidence now to deny it. You will agree, sir?

PROCTOR. (*Evading.*) I . . . have no knowledge in that line. But it's hard to think so pious a woman be secretly a Devil's bitch after seventy year of such good prayer.

HALE. Aye. But the Devil is a wily one, you cannot deny it. However, she is far from accused, and I know she will not be. I thought, sir, to put some questions as to the Christian character of this house, if you'll permit me.

PROCTOR. Why, we . . . have no fear of questions, sir.

HALE. Good, then. In the book of record that Mister Parris keeps, I note that you are rarely in the church on Sabbath Day. . . .

PROCTOR. No, sir, you are mistaken. . . .

HALE. Only twenty-six time in seventeen month, sir. I must call that rare. Will you tell me why you are so absent?

PROCTOR. Mister Hale, (*Slight pause as he controls himself.*) I never knew I must account to that man for I come to church or stay at home. . . . My wife were sick this winter.

HALE. (*Kindly.*) So I am told. But you, Mister, why could you not come alone?

PROCTOR. I surely did come when I could, and when I could not I prayed in this house.

HALE. Mister Proctor, your house is not a church; your theology must tell you that.

PROCTOR. (*Restraining his anger.*) It does, sir, it does; and it tells me that a minister may pray to God without he have golden candlesticks upon the altar.

HALE. What golden candlesticks . . . ?

PROCTOR. (*A pause. His L. hand gripping edge of table as he controls his anger.*) Since we built the church there were pewter candlesticks upon the altar; Francis Nurse made them, y'know, and a sweeter hand never touched the metal. But Parris came, and for *twenty week* he preach nothing but golden candlesticks until he had them. I labor the earth from dawn of day to blink of night, and I tell you *true*, when I look to heaven and see my money glaring at his elbows—it—it hurt my prayer, sir, it hurt my prayer. I think, sometimes, the man dreams *cathedrals*, not clapboard meeting houses.

HALE. And yet, Mister, a Christian on Sabbath Day must be in church. . . . Tell me—you have three children.

PROCTOR. Aye. Boys.

HALE. How come it that only *two* are baptized?

PROCTOR. (*Pauses as he controls himself and looks at Elizabeth. Uncomfortable at the thought.*) I like it not that Mister Parris should lay his hand upon my baby. I see no light of God in that man. I'll not conceal it.

HALE. I must say it, Mister Proctor; that is not for you to decide. The man's ordained, therefore the light of God is in him.

PROCTOR. What's your suspicion, Mister Hale?

37

HALE. No—no, I have no . . .

PROCTOR. I nailed the roof upon the church, I hung the door . . .

HALE. (*Eagerly.*) Oh, did you! That's a good sign, then.

PROCTOR. It may be I have been too quick to bring the man to book, but you cannot think we *ever* desired the destruction of religion. I think that's in your mind, is it not?

HALE. I . . . have . . . there is a softness in your record, sir, a softness.

ELIZABETH. I think, maybe, we *have* been too hard with Mister Parris. I think so. But sure we never loved the Devil here.

HALE. Do you know your commandments, Elizabeth?

ELIZABETH. (*Without hesitation, simply, primly.*) I surely do. There be no mark of blame upon my life, Mister Hale, I am a covenanted Christian woman.

HALE. And you, Mister?

PROCTOR. I . . . am sure I do, sir.

HALE. Let you repeat them, if you will.

PROCTOR. . . . The Commandments?

HALE. Aye.

PROCTOR. Thou shalt not kill.

HALE. Aye.

PROCTOR. Thou shalt not steal. Thou shalt not covet thy neighbor's goods, nor make unto thee any graven image. Thou shalt not take the name of the Lord in vain; thou shalt have no other gods before me . . . thou shalt remember the Sabbath Day and keep it holy. Thou shalt honor thy father and mother. Thou shalt not bear false witness. Thou shalt not make unto thee any graven image.

HALE. You have said that twice, sir.

PROCTOR. Aye.

ELIZABETH. (*Delicately.*) Adultery, John.

PROCTOR. (*As though a secret arrow had pained his heart.*) Aye! (*Trying to grin it away—to Hale.*) You see, sir, between the two of us we do know them all. (*Hale only looks at Proctor, deep in his attempt to define this man. Proctor grows more uneasy.*) I think it be a small fault.

HALE. (*Thoughtfully and regretfully.*) Theology, sir, is a fortress; no crack in a fortress may be accounted small.

PROCTOR. There be no love for Satan in *this* house.

HALE. I pray it, I pray it dearly. (*Rising.*) Well, then, I'll bid you good night.

ELIZABETH. (*Unable to restrain her anxiety.*) Mister Hale. I do think you are suspecting me somewhat? Are you not?

HALE. Goody Proctor, I do not judge you. My duty is to add what I may to the Godly wisdom of the court. I pray you both good health and good fortune. Good night, sir. (*Starts out* R.)

ELIZABETH. (*With a note of desperation.*) I think you must *tell* him, John.

HALE. What's that?

ELIZABETH. Will you tell him?

PROCTOR. I . . . I have no witness and cannot prove it, except my word be taken. But I know the children's sickness had naught to do with witchcraft.

HALE. (*Stopped, struck.*) Naught to do . . . ?

PROCTOR. They were discovered by Mr. Parris sporting in the woods. They were startled, and took sick.

HALE. Who told you this?

PROCTOR. Abigail Williams.

HALE. Abigail!

PROCTOR. Aye.

HALE. Abigail Williams said it had naught to do with witchcraft?

PROCTOR. She told me the day you came, sir.

HALE. Why . . . why did you keep this?

PROCTOR. I never knew until *tonight* that the world is gone daft with this nonsense.

HALE. Nonsense! Mister, I have myself examined Tituba, Sarah Good and numerous others that have confessed to dealing with the Devil. They have *confessed* it.

PROCTOR. (*With dry, bitter humor.*) And why not, if they must hang for denyin' it? There are them that will swear to anything before they'll hang; have you never thought of *that?*

HALE. (*It is his own suspicion, but he resists it.*) I have. I . . . I have indeed. And you . . . would you testify to this in *court?*

PROCTOR. I . . . . had not reckoned with going into court. . . . But if I *must* I *will.*

HALE. Ah, you falter there? I think you . . .

PROCTOR. (*Controlling himself.*) . . . I falter nothing, but I . . . I may wonder if my story will be credited in such a court. I do wonder on it, when a minister as steady minded as you will

39

suspicion such a woman that never lied; she cannot lie, and the world knows she cannot. I may falter somewhat, Mister, I am no fool.

HALE. (*Quietly—it has impressed him.*) Proctor, let you open with me now, for I have heard a thing that troubles me. It's said you hold no belief that there may even be witches in the world. Is that true, sir?

PROCTOR. I know not what I have said; I may have said it. I have wondered if there be witches in the world.

HALE. Then you do not believe . . . ?

PROCTOR. I have no knowledge of it; the Bible speaks of witches, and I will not *deny them.*

HALE. And you, woman?

ELIZABETH. I . . . I cannot believe it.

HALE. (*Shocked.*) You cannot!

PROCTOR. Elizabeth, you bewilder him!

ELIZABETH. (*To Hale. Angrily.*) I cannot think the Devil may own a woman's soul, Mister Hale, when she keeps an upright way, as I have. I am a good woman, I know it; and if you believe I may do only good work in the world, and yet be secretly bound to Satan, then I must tell you, sir, I do not believe it.

HALE. But, woman, you do believe there are witches in . . . ?

ELIZABETH. If you think that I am one, then I say there are none.

HALE. You surely do not fly against the Gospel, the Gospel . . .

PROCTOR. She believe in the Gospel, every word!

ELIZABETH. Question Abigail Williams about the Gospel, not myself!

PROCTOR. She do not mean to doubt the Gospel, sir, you cannot think it. This be a Christian house, sir, a Christian house.

HALE. (*Sighing.*) God keep you both; let the third child be quickly baptized and go you without fail each Sunday into Sabbath prayer; and keep a solemn, quiet way among you. I think . . .
(*Enter Corey,* R.)

COREY. John!

PROCTOR. Giles! What's the matter?

COREY. They take my wife. And Rebecca Nurse! (*Nurse enters* R.)

PROCTOR. (*To Nurse.*) Rebecca's in the *jail!*

NURSE. John, Cheever come and take her in his wagon. We've

40

only now come from the jail and they'll not even let us in to see them.

ELIZABETH. They've surely gone wild now, Mister Hale!

NURSE. Reverend Hale. Can you not speak to the Deputy Governor?—I'm sure he mistakes these people . . .

HALE. Pray calm yourself, Mister Nurse. . . .

NURSE. My wife is the very brick and mortar of the church, Mister Hale—and Martha Corey, there cannot be a woman closer yet to God than Martha.

HALE. (*Incredulously.*) How is Rebecca charged, Mr. Nurse?

NURSE. For *murder*, she's charged! "For the marvelous and supernatural murder of Goody Putnam's babies." What am I to do, Mr. Hale?

HALE. Believe me, sir, if Rebecca Nurse be tainted, then nothing's left to stop the whole green world from burning. Let you rest upon the justice of the court; the court will send her home, I know it . . .

NURSE. You cannot mean she will be tried in court!

PROCTOR. How may such a woman murder children?

HALE. Man, remember, until an hour before the Devil fell, God thought him beautiful in Heaven.

COREY. I never said my wife were a witch, Mister Hale, I only said she were reading books!

HALE. Mister Corey, exactly what complaint were made on your wife?

COREY. That bloody mongrel Wallcott charge her. Y' see, he buy a pig of my wife four or five year ago, and the pig died soon after. So he come dancin' in for his money back. So my Martha she says to him, "Wallcott, if you haven't the wit to feed a pig properly, you'll not live to own many," she says. Now he goes to court and claims that from that day to this he cannot keep a pig alive for more than four weeks because my Martha bewitch them with her books! (*Enter Cheever R.*)

CHEEVER. Good evening. Good evening to you, John Proctor. (*Willard enters* R., *to just inside door.*)

PROCTOR. Why . . . Mister Cheever. Good evening.

CHEEVER. Good evening, all. Good evening, Mister Hale.

PROCTOR. I hope you come not on business of the court?

CHEEVER. I do, Proctor, aye. I am clerk of the court now, y'know.

41

COREY. It's a pity, Ezekiel, that an honest tailor might have gone to heaven must burn in hell. You'll burn for this, do you know it?

CHEEVER. You know yourself I must do as I'm told. You surely know that, Giles. And I'd as lief you'd not be sending me to hell. I like not the sound of it, I tell you, I like not the sound of it. Now believe me, Proctor, how heavy be the law, all its tonnage I do carry on my back tonight. . . . (*Takes a warrant from pocket.*) I have a warrant for your wife.

PROCTOR. What say you? A warrant for my wife? (*To Hale.*) You said she were not charged!

HALE. (*Confounded.*) I know nothin' of it. (*To Cheever.*) When were she charged?

CHEEVER. I am given sixteen warrant tonight, sir, and she is one.

PROCTOR. (*To Cheever.*) Who charged her?

CHEEVER. Why, Abigail Williams charge her.

PROCTOR. Abigail Williams? On what proof, what proof!

CHEEVER. Mister Proctor, I have little time. . . . The court bid me search your house, but I like not to search a house. So will you hand me any poppets that your wife may keep here.

PROCTOR. Poppets?

ELIZABETH. I never kept no poppets, not since I were a girl.

CHEEVER. I spy a poppet, Goody Proctor.

ELIZABETH. (*Gets doll.*) Oh!—Why, this is Mary's.

CHEEVER. Would you please to give it to me?

ELIZABETH. (*Handing doll to Cheever.*) Has the court discovered a text in poppets now?

CHEEVER. (*Carefully holds doll.*) Do you keep any others in this house?

PROCTOR. No, nor this one either till tonight. What signifies a poppet?

CHEEVER. Why, a poppet . . . a poppet may signify. Now, woman . . . will you please to come with me.

PROCTOR. She will not. (*To Elizabeth.*) Fetch Mary here.

CHEEVER. No—no, I am forbid to leave her from my sight.

PROCTOR. You'll leave her out of sight and out of mind, Mister. Fetch Mary, Elizabeth. (*Elizabeth goes out D. L.*)

HALE. (*Bewildered.*) What signifies a poppet, Mister Cheever?

CHEEVER. (*Turns doll over in his hands.*) Why, they say it may signify that she . . . (*He has lifted doll's skirt, and his eyes widen in astonished fear.*) Why, this, this . . .

PROCTOR. What's there?

CHEEVER. Why . . . (*Draws out a long needle from doll.*) it is a needle! Willard, Willard, it is a needle!

PROCTOR. And what signifies a needle!

CHEEVER. Why, this go hard with her, Proctor, this . . . I had my doubts, Proctor, I had my doubts, but here's calamity. . . . (*Crosses to Hale, shows needle.*) You see it, sir, it is a needle!

HALE. Why? What meanin' has it?

CHEEVER. The girl, the Williams girl, Abigail Williams, sir. She sat to dinner in Reverend Parris' house tonight, and without word nor warnin', she falls to the floor. Like a struck beast, he says, and screamed a scream that a bull would weep to hear. And he goes to save her, and stuck two inches in the flesh of her belly he draw a needle out. And demandin' of her how she come to be so stabbed, she . . . (*To Proctor.*) testify it were your wife's familiar spirit pushed it in.

PROCTOR. Why, she done it herself! I hope you're not takin' this for proof, Mister Hale.

CHEEVER. 'Tis hard proof!—I find here a poppet Goody Proctor keeps. I have found it, sir. And in the belly of the poppet a needle stuck. I tell you true, Proctor, I never warranted to *see* such proof of Hell, and I bid you obstruct me not, for I . . . (*Enter Elizabeth with Mary.*)

PROCTOR. Here now! Mary, how did this poppet come into my house?

MARY. What poppet's that, sir?

PROCTOR. This poppet, this poppet.

MARY. (*Looks at it, and evasively says.*) Why, I . . . I think it is mine.

PROCTOR. (*A threat.*) It is your poppet, is it not?

MARY. It . . . is, sir.

PROCTOR. And how did it come into this house?

MARY. Why . . . I made it in the court, sir, and . . . give it to Goody Proctor tonight.

PROCTOR. (*To Hale.*) Now, sir—do you have it?

HALE. Mary Warren . . . a needle have been found inside this poppet.

MARY. Why, I meant no harm by it, sir. . . .

PROCTOR. You stuck that needle in yourself?

MARY. I . . . I believe I did, sir, I . . .

PROCTOR. (*To Hale.*) What say you now?

HALE. (*Still kindly endeavoring to get at the truth.*) Child . . . you are certain this be your natural memory?—may it be, perhaps, that someone conjures you even *now* to say this?

MARY. Conjures me?—Why, no, sir, I am entirely myself, I think. Let you ask Susanna Wallcott—she saw me sewin' it in court. Ask *Abby*, Abby sat beside me when I made it.

PROCTOR. (*To Hale, of Cheever.*) Bid him begone, Mister. Your mind is surely settled now. Bid him out, Mister.

ELIZABETH. (*Bewildered.*) What signifies a *needle*?

HALE. Mary . . . you charge a cold and cruel murder on Abigail.

MARY. Murder! I charge no . . .

HALE. Abigail were stabbed tonight; a needle were found stuck into her belly. . . .

ELIZABETH. And she charges *me*?!

HALE. Aye.

ELIZABETH. Why . . . !—The girl is murder! She must be ripped out of the world!

CHEEVER. You've heard that, sir!—Ripped out of the world! Willard, you heard it! . . .

PROCTOR. (*Suddenly snatches warrant out of Cheever's hands.*) Out with you!

CHEEVER. Proctor, you dare not touch the warrant. . . .

PROCTOR. (*Rips warrant.*) Out with you!

CHEEVER. You've ripped the Deputy Governor's warrant, man!

PROCTOR. Damn the Deputy Governor! Out of my house!

HALE. Now, Proctor, Proctor . . .

PROCTOR. (*To Hale.*) Get y' gone with them! You are a broken minister.

HALE. Proctor, if she is innocent the court . . .

PROCTOR. If *she* is innocent! Why do you never wonder if Parris be innocent, or Abigail? Is the accuser always holy now? Were they born this morning as clean as God's fingers? I'll tell you what's walking Salem—vengeance is walking Salem. We are what we always were in Salem, but now the little crazy children are jangling the keys of the kingdom, and common vengeance writes the law! This warrant's vengeance; I will not give my wife to vengeance!

ELIZABETH. I'll go, John . . .

44

PROCTOR. You will *not* go! (*Sweeps his gun up, pointing it at Cheever.*)

WILLARD. John, I have nine men outside. You cannot keep her. The law binds me, John, I cannot budge.

PROCTOR. (*To Hale.*) You will see her taken?

HALE. Proctor, the court is just. . . .

PROCTOR. Pontius Pilate! God will not let you wash your hands of this!

ELIZABETH. John . . . (*She presses the rifle down.*) I think I must go with them. (*Taking off apron, handing it to Mary.*) Mary . . . there is bread enough for the morning; you will bake in the afternoon. Help Mister Proctor as you were his daughter . . . you owe me that, and much more. (*Takes Proctor's hand. To Proctor. . . .*) When the children wake, speak nothing of witchcraft . . . it will frighten them. . . .

PROCTOR. (*Taking her hands.*) I will bring you home. I will bring you soon.

ELIZABETH. Oh, John, bring me soon!

PROCTOR. I will fall like an ocean on that court! Fear nothing, Elizabeth.

ELIZABETH. I will fear nothing. (*Takes shawl from wash stand, he puts it on her. They cross R. Cheever and Willard exit R.*) Tell the children I have gone to visit someone sick. . . . (*She breaks off, goes out R. Hale sits bench R. of table, head bowed in L. hand, his L. hand on table. After four seconds chains are heard off R.*)

PROCTOR. (*Running off R.*) Willard! Willard, don't chain her! Damn you, man, you will not chain her! (*Outside.*) Off with them! I'll not have it! I will not have her chained! (*And other men's voices against his. Corey calls to Hale.*)

COREY. And yet silent, Minister? It is fraud, you know it is fraud! What keeps you, man! (*Proctor is thrown into room by two guards, followed by Willard. Guards exit R. after Proctor pulls away.*)

PROCTOR. I'll pay you, Willard, I will surely pay you! (*Sits bench R., head in hands.*)

WILLARD. In God's name, John, I cannot help myself. I must chain them all. Now let you keep inside this house till I am gone! (*To Hale.*) Man, are you blind? (*He exits R.*)

HALE. Mister Proctor . . .

45

PROCTOR. (*His weeping heart pressing his words.*) Out of my sight!

HALE. (*Pleading.*) Charity, Proctor, *Charity*—what I have heard in her favor I will not fear to˙ testify in court. God help me, I cannot judge her guilty nor innocent. . . . I know not. Only this consider—the world goes mad, and it profit nothing you should lay the cause to the vengeance of a little girl.

PROCTOR. You are a coward! Though you be ordained in God's own tears, you are a coward now!

HALE. (*Shaken. Greatly disturbed, trying to convince himself.*) Proctor, I cannot think God be provoked so grandly by such a *petty* cause. The jails are packed, our greatest judges sit in Salem now—and hangin's promised. Man, we must look to cause proportionate. Were there murder done perhaps, and never brought to light? Abomination? Some secret blasphemy that stinks to heaven? Think on cause, man, and let you help me to discover it. For there's your way, believe it, there is your only way, when such confusion strikes upon the world. (*Crossing to Nurse. Pleading with them.*) Let you counsel among yourselves; think on your village, and what may have drawn from heaven such thundering wrath upon you all. I shall pray God open up our eyes. (*Hale goes out* R.)

NURSE. I never heard no murder done in Salem.

PROCTOR. Leave me, Francis, leave me. (*Nurse slowly exits* R.)

COREY. John . . . tell me, are we lost?

PROCTOR. Go home now, Giles. We'll speak on it tomorrow.

COREY. Let you think on it; we'll come early, eh?

PROCTOR. Aye. Go now, Giles.

COREY. Good night, then. (*Corey goes out* R. *Long pause.*)

MARY. Mister Proctor, very likely they'll let her come home once they're given proper evidence.

PROCTOR. You're coming to the court with me, Mary. You will tell it in the court.

MARY. I cannot charge murder on Abigail. . . .

PROCTOR. You will tell the court how that poppet come here and who stuck the needle in.

MARY. She'll kill me for sayin' that! Abby'll charge lechery on you, Mister Proctor!

PROCTOR. (*Stops.*) . . . She's told you!

MARY. I have known it, sir. She'll ruin you with it, I know she will.

PROCTOR. (*Advancing on her.*) Good. Then her saintliness is done with. We will slide together into our pit. You will tell the court what you know.

MARY. I cannot. They'll turn on me.

PROCTOR. (*Grabs her.*) My wife will never die for me. I will bring your guts into your mouth, but that goodness will not die for me.

MARY. I cannot do it. I cannot.

PROCTOR. Make your peace with it. Now Hell and Heaven grapple on our backs, and all our old pretense is ripped away. Make your peace. (*Throws her down.*)

MARY. (*Sobs.*) I cannot.

PROCTOR. (*Crossing to door* L.) Peace! It is a Providence and no great change. We are what we always were, but naked now. Aye, naked. And the wind, God's icy wind, will blow. (*Mary continues sobbing, "I cannot!"*)

CURTAIN

ACT II

Scene 1

SCENE: *A wood. Night. Light is concentrated on log*
D. S. L.

Proctor enters D. L. *with lantern, glancing behind him,
then halts, holding lantern raised. Abigail appears* D. L.
*with a wrap over her nightgown, her hair down. A mo-
ment of questioning silence.*

PROCTOR. (*Searching. Crosses to* D. R. *of log.*) I must speak
with you, Abigail. (*She does not move, staring at him.*) Will you
sit?

ABIGAIL. How do you come?

PROCTOR. Friendly.

ABIGAIL. (*Glancing about.*) I don't like the woods at night.
Pray you, stand closer. (*He comes closer to her.*) I knew it must
be you. When I heard the pebbles on the window, before I opened
up my eyes I knew. (*Sits on* L. *of log.*) I thought you would come a
good time sooner.

PROCTOR. I had thought to come many times.

ABIGAIL. Why didn't you? I am so alone in the world now.

PROCTOR. (*As a fact. Not bitterly.*) Are you! I've heard that
people ride a hundred mile to see your face these days.

ABIGAIL. Aye, my face. Can you see my face?

PROCTOR. (*Holds lantern to her face.*) Then you're troubled?

ABIGAIL. Have you come to mock me?

PROCTOR. (*Sets lantern on ground. Sits next to her.*) No, no,
but I hear only that you go to the tavern every night, and play
shovelboard with the Deputy Governor, and they give you cider.

ABIGAIL. I have once or twice played the shovelboard. But I have
no joy in it.

PROCTOR. This is a surprise, Abby. I'd thought to find you gayer
than this. I'm told a troop of boys go step for step with you
wherever you walk these days.

ABIGAIL. Aye, they do. But I have only lewd looks from the boys.

PROCTOR. And you like that not?

ABIGAIL. I cannot bear lewd looks no more, John. My spirit's changed entirely. I ought be given Godly looks when I suffer for them as I do.

PROCTOR. Oh? How do you suffer, Abby?

ABIGAIL. (*Pulls up dress.*) Why, look at my leg. I'm holes all over from their damned needles and pins. (*Touching her stomach.*) The jab your wife gave me's not healed yet, y'know.

PROCTOR. (*Seeing her madness now.*) Oh, it isn't.

ABIGAIL. I think sometimes she pricks it open again while I sleep.

PROCTOR. Ah?

ABIGAIL. And George Jacobs—(*Sliding up her sleeve.*) he comes again and again and raps me with his stick—the same spot every night all this week. Look at the lump I have.

PROCTOR. Abby—George Jacobs is in the jail all this month.

ABIGAIL. Thank God he is, and bless the day he hangs and lets me sleep in peace again! Oh, John, the world's so full of hypocrites! (*Astonished, outraged.*) They pray in jail! I'm told they all pray in jail!

PROCTOR. They may not pray?

ABIGAIL. And torture me in my bed while sacred words are comin' from their mouths? Oh, it will need God Himself to cleanse this town properly!

PROCTOR. Abby—you mean to cry out still others?

ABIGAIL. (*Front.*) If I live, if I am not murdered, I surely will, until the last hypocrite is dead.

PROCTOR. Then there is no one good?

ABIGAIL. Aye, there is one. *You* are good.

PROCTOR. Am I! How am I good?

ABIGAIL. Why, you taught me goodness, therefore you are good. It were a fire you walked me through, and all my ignorance was burned away. It were a fire, John, we lay in fire. And from that night no woman dare call me wicked any more but I knew my answer. I used to weep for my sins when the wind lifted up my skirts; and blushed for shame because some old Rebecca called me loose. And then you burned my ignorance away. As bare as some December tree I saw them all—walking like saints to church, running to feed the sick, and hypocrites in their hearts! And God gave me strength to call them liars, and God made men to listen to me, and by God I will scrub the world clean for the love of

49

Him! Oh, John, I will make you such a wife when the world is white again! (*She kisses his hand.*) You will be amazed to see me every day, a light of heaven in your house, a —— (*He rises, backs away, amazed.*) Why are you cold?

PROCTOR. My wife goes to trial in the morning, Abigail.

ABIGAIL. (*Distantly.*) Your wife?

PROCTOR. Surely you knew of it?

ABIGAIL. I do remember it now. How—how —— Is she well?

PROCTOR. As well as she may be, thirty-six days in that place.

ABIGAIL. You said you came friendly.

PROCTOR. She will not be condemned, Abby.

ABIGAIL. You brought me from my bed to speak of her?

PROCTOR. I come to tell you, Abby, what I will do tomorrow in the court. I would not take you by surprise, but give you all good time to think on what to do to save yourself.

ABIGAIL. Save myself!

PROCTOR. If you do not free my wife tomorrow, I am set and bound to ruin you, Abby.

ABIGAIL. (*Her voice small—astonished.*) How—ruin me?

PROCTOR. I have rocky proof in documents that you knew that poppet were none of my wife's; and that you yourself bade Mary Warren stab that needle into it.

ABIGAIL. (*A wildness stirs in her, a child is standing here who is unutterably frustrated, denied her wish, but she is still grasping for her wits.*) I bade Mary Warren ——?

PROCTOR. You know what you do, you are not so mad!

ABIGAIL. Oh, hypocrites! Have you won him, too?! John, why do you let them send you?

PROCTOR. I warn you, Abby!

ABIGAIL. They send you! They steal your honesty and ——

PROCTOR. I have found my honesty!

ABIGAIL. No, this is your wife pleading, your snivelling, envious wife! This is Rebecca's voice, Martha Corey's voice. You were no hypocrite!

PROCTOR. I will prove you for the fraud you are!

ABIGAIL. And if they ask you why Abigail would ever do so murderous a deed, what will you tell them?

PROCTOR. I will tell them why.

ABIGAIL. What will you tell? You will confess to fornication? In the court?

PROCTOR. If you will have it so, so I will tell it! (*She utters a disbelieving laugh.*) I say I will! (*She laughs louder, now with more assurance he will never do it. He shakes her roughly.*) If you can still hear, hear this! Can you hear! (*She is trembling, staring up at him as though he were out of his mind.*) You will tell the court you are blind to spirits; you cannot see them any more, and you will never cry witchery again, or I will make you famous for the whore you are!

ABIGAIL. (*Grabs him.*) Never in this world! I know you, John—you are this moment singing secret Hallelujahs that your wife will hang!

PROCTOR. (*Throws her down.*) You mad, you murderous bitch!

ABIGAIL. Oh, how hard it is when pretense falls! But it falls, it falls! (*She wraps herself up as though to go.*) You have done your duty by her. I hope it is your last hypocrisy. I pray you will come again with sweeter news for me. I know you will—now that your duty's done. Good night, John. (*She is backing away L., raising her hand in farewell.*) Fear naught. I will save you tomorrow. (*As she turns and goes D. L.*) From yourself I will save you. (*She is gone D. L. Proctor is left alone, amazed, in terror. Takes up his lantern and slowly exits U. L. as lights dim out and curtain falls.*)

CURTAIN

ACT II

SCENE 2

The vestry room of the Meeting House. There are 3 entrances: one at D. L. leading to outside; one at D. R. leading to courtroom and one at U. R. leading to the judges' chambers. In the Meeting House proper, beyond the R. wall, offstage, an examination is going on as curtain rises. The stage is empty, but we hear offstage . . .

HATHORNE. Now, Martha Corey, there is abundant evidence in our hands to show that you have given yourself to the reading of fortunes. Do you deny it?

51

MARTHA. I am innocent to a witch. I know not what a witch is.

HATHORNE. How do you know then that you are not a witch?

MARTHA. If I were I would know it.

HATHORNE. Why do you hurt these children?

MARTHA. I do not hurt them. I scorn it!

COREY. I have evidence for the court! (*Voices of townsfolk rise in excitement.*)

DANFORTH. You will keep your seat!

COREY. Thomas Putnam is reachin' out for land! (*Crowd louder.*)

DANFORTH. Remove that man, Marshal! (*A roaring goes up from the people.*)

COREY. You're hearing lies, lies!

HATHORNE. Arrest him, Excellency!

COREY. I have evidence, why will you not hear my evidence! (*Corey is half-carried into this vestry room by Willard, followed by Parris, all come from D. R.*) Hands off, damn you, let me go!

WILLARD. Giles, Giles . . . !

COREY. (*To Willard who is pulling him across stage.*) Out of my way, Willard! I bring evidence. . . .

WILLARD. You cannot go in there, Giles—it's a court!

HALE. (*Entering D. R., going after them.*) Pray be calm a moment.

COREY. You, Mr. Hale, go in there and demand I speak.

HALE. A moment, sir, a moment.

COREY. They'll be hangin' my wife —— (*Hathorne enters D. R. Nurse enters D. R. after Hathorne.*)

HATHORNE. How do you dare come roarin' into this court! Are you gone daft, Corey? (*Crowd subsides.*)

COREY. You're not a Boston judge yet, Hathorne. You'll not call me daft! (*Enter Deputy Governor Danforth and behind him, Ezekiel Cheever U. R. Silence falls. Danforth is a grave man in his sixties, of some humor and sophistication that does not, however, interfere with an exact loyalty to his position and his cause.*)

DANFORTH. (*Looking at Corey.*) Who is this man?

PARRIS. Giles Corey, sir, and a more contentious . . .

COREY. (*To Parris.*) I am asked the question and I am old enough to answer it! (*To Danforth.*) My name is Corey, sir, Giles Corey. I have six hundred acres, and timber in addition. It is my wife you be condemning now. (*He indicates the courtroom D. R.*)

DANFORTH. And how do you imagine to help her cause with

such contemptuous riot? Now begone, your old age alone keeps you out of jail for this.

COREY. They're tellin' lies about my wife, sir, I . . .

DANFORTH. Then you take it upon yourself to decide what this court shall believe and what it shall set aside?

COREY. Your Excellency, we mean no disrespect for . . .

DANFORTH. Disrespect, indeed!—It is disruption, Mister. This is the highest court of the supreme government of this province, do you know it?

COREY. (*He is beginning to weep.*) Your Excellency, I only said she were readin' books, sir, and they come and take her out of my house for . . .

DANFORTH. What books, what . . . ?

COREY. (*Through helpless sobs.*) It is my third wife, sir, and I never had no wife that be so taken with books, d'y'understand, sir, and I thought to find the cause of it, d'y'see, but it were no witch I blamed her for. . . . (*He is openly weeping.*) I have broke charity with the woman, I have broke charity with her. (*He covers his face, ashamed. Danforth is respectfully silent.*)

HALE. Excellency, he claims hard evidence for his wife's defense. I think that in all justice you must . . .

DANFORTH. Then let him submit his evidence in proper affidavit. You are certainly aware of our procedure here, Mr. Hale. (*To Willard.*) Clear this room.

WILLARD. Come now, Giles. (*Gently pushes Corey out* D. L.)

NURSE. We are desperate, sir; we come here three days now and cannot be heard.

DANFORTH. Who is this man?

NURSE. Francis Nurse, your Excellency.

HALE. His wife's Rebecca that were condemned this morning.

DANFORTH. Indeed! I am amazed to find you in such uproar— I have only good report of your character, Mister Nurse.

HATHORNE. I think they must both be arrested in contempt, sir.

DANFORTH. (*To Nurse.*) Let you write your plea and in due time I will . . .

NURSE. Excellency, we have *proof* for your eyes, God forbid you shut them to it. The girls, sir, the girls are frauds.

DANFORTH. (*With interest.*) What's what?

NURSE. We have proof of it, sir. They are all deceiving you.

HATHORNE. This is contempt, sir, contempt!

53

DANFORTH. Peace, Judge Hathorne. Do you know who I am, Mister Nurse?

NURSE. (*Respectfully.*) I surely do, sir, and I think you must be a wise judge to be what you are.

DANFORTH. (*Deliberately.*) And do you know that near to four hundred are in the jails from Marblehead to Lynn, and upon my signature?

NURSE. I . . .

DANFORTH. And seventy-two condemned to hang by that signature?

NURSE. (*With deference but emphasis.*) Excellency, I never thought to say it to such a weighty judge, but you are deceived. (*All turn to see Mary Warren enter* D. L. *with Proctor and Corey. Mary is keeping her eyes to the ground, Proctor has her elbow as though she were breakable.*)

PARRIS. (*In shock.*) Mary Warren! What, what are you about here?

PROCTOR. She would speak with the Deputy-Governor.

DANFORTH. (*To Willard.*) Did you not tell me Mary Warren were sick in bed?

WILLARD. She were, Your Honor—when I go to fetch her to the court last week, she said she were sick.

COREY. She has been strivin' with her soul *all* week, Your Honor; she comes now to tell the *truth* to you.

DANFORTH. Who is this?

PROCTOR. (*Unafraid.*) John Proctor, sir. Elizabeth Proctor is my wife.

PARRIS. Beware this man, Your Excellency, this man is mischief.

HALE. (*With great urgency.*) I think you must hear the girl, sir, she . . .

DANFORTH. (*He has become very interested in Mary Warren and only raises a hand toward Hale.*) Peace. What would you tell us, Mary Warren?

PROCTOR. (*He and Mary Warren step forward.*) She never saw no spirits, sir.

DANFORTH. (*With great alarm and surprise, to Mary.*) Never saw no spirits?!

COREY. (*Eagerly.*) Never.

PROCTOR. (*Has three papers in his hand.*) She has signed a deposition, sir. . . .

54

DANFORTH. No, no, I accept no depositions. Tell me, Mister Proctor, have you given out this story in the village?

PROCTOR. We have not.

PARRIS. They've come to overthrow the court, sir! This man is . . .

DANFORTH. I pray you, Mister Parris. Do you know, Mister Proctor, that the entire contention of the State in these trials is that the voice of Heaven is speaking through the children?

PROCTOR. I know that, sir.

DANFORTH. And you, Mary Warren . . . how came you to cry out people for sending their spirits against you?

MARY. (Between Corey and Proctor.) It were pretense, sir.

DANFORTH. I cannot hear you.

PROCTOR. It were pretense, she says.

DANFORTH. (With great unbelief.) Ah? And the other girls? Susanna Wallcott, and . . . the others? They are also pretending?

MARY. Aye, sir.

DANFORTH. Indeed. Now, Mister Proctor, before I decide whether I shall hear you or not, it is my duty to tell you this. We burn a hot fire here; it melts down all concealment. Are you certain in your conscience, Mister, that your evidence is the truth?

PROCTOR. It is. And you will surely know it.

DANFORTH. I take it you came here to declare this revelation in the open court before the public?

PROCTOR. I thought I would, aye . . . with your permission.

DANFORTH. Now, sir—what is your purpose in so doing?

PROCTOR. Why, I . . . I would free my wife, sir . . .

DANFORTH. There lurks nowhere in your heart, nor hidden in your spirit, any desire to undermine this court?

PROCTOR. Why, no, sir.

DANFORTH. (With an implied threat.) I tell you straight, Mister —I have seen marvels in this court. I have seen people choked before my eyes by spirits, I have seen them stuck by pins and slashed by daggers. I have until this moment not the slightest reason to suspect that the children may be deceiving me. Do you understand my meaning?

PROCTOR. (Eagerly.) Excellency, does it not strike upon you that so many of these women have lived so long with such upright reputation, and . . .

PARRIS. Do you read the Gospel, Mister Proctor?

PROCTOR. I read the Gospel.

PARRIS. (*Smugly.*) I think *not*, or you should surely know that Cain were an upright man and yet he did kill *Abel*.

PROCTOR. Aye, God tells us that. But who tells us Rebecca Nurse *murdered* seven babies by sending out her spirit on them? It is the children only, and this one will swear she lied to you.

DANFORTH. Judge Hathorne! (*Danforth leans across table, to Hathorne, whispers to him. Hathorne nods.*)

HATHORNE. Aye, she's the one.

DANFORTH. Mister Proctor . . . this morning, your wife sent me a claim in which she states that she is pregnant now.

PROCTOR. My wife pregnant!

DANFORTH. There be no sign of it—we have examined her body.

PROCTOR. But if she say she is pregnant, then she must be! That woman will never lie, Mister Danforth.

DANFORTH. She will not?

PROCTOR. Never, sir, never.

DANFORTH. Mister Proctor, if I should tell you now that I will let her be kept another month; and if she begin to show her natural signs, you shall have her living yet another *year* until she is delivered—(*Looks at Proctor.*) what say you to that? (*Proctor is struck silent.*) Come now. You say your only purpose is to save your wife. Good then, she is saved at least this year, and a year is long. What say you, sir? (*Claps hands.*) It is done now. Will you drop this charge? (*Proctor thinks, looks at Corey.*)

PROCTOR. I . . . I think I cannot.

DANFORTH. Then your purpose is somewhat larger?

PARRIS. (*Triumphantly.*) He's come to overthrow this court, Your Honor!

PROCTOR. (*Sincerely.*) These are my friends. Their wives are also . . .

DANFORTH. (*A sudden change of manner.*) I judge you not, sir. Sit down. I am ready to hear your evidence. (*Nurse crosses* L. *to Corey, talks to him.*)

PROCTOR. (*Crossing, puts Mary on stool* L. *of table.*) I come not to hurt the court, I only . . . (*Proctor crosses* D. L., *talks with Corey and Nurse.*)

DANFORTH. Marshal, go into the Court and bid Judge Stoughton and Judge Sewall declare recess for one hour. And let them go to the tavern, if they will. All witnesses and prisoners are to be kept in the building.

WILLARD. (*To Danforth.*) If you'll forgive me, sir, I've known him all my life. It is a good man, sir.

DANFORTH. I'm sure of it, Marshal. (*Willard exits D. R. Danforth crosses up above table to C. chair. Parris pulls chair out. Danforth sits, puts on glasses.*) Now what deposition do you have for us, Mister Proctor? And I beg you be clear, open as the sky, and honest.

PROCTOR. I am no lawyer, so I'll . . .

DANFORTH. The pure in heart need no lawyers. Proceed as you will.

PROCTOR. (*Handing Danforth paper.*) Will you read this first, sir? It's a sort of testament. The people signing it declare their good opinion of Rebecca and my wife, and Martha Corey. (*Danforth looks at paper.*)

PARRIS. Their good opinion! (*Danforth goes on reading.*)

PROCTOR. These are all *covenant people,* landholding farmers, members of the church. (*Delicately, trying to point out a paragraph.*) If you'll notice, sir—they've known the women many years and never saw no sign they had dealings with the Devil.

DANFORTH. (*Glancing at long list.*) How many names are here?

FRANCIS. Ninety-one, Your Excellency.

PARRIS. These people should be summoned for questioning.

NURSE. (*Alarmed.*) Mister Danforth, I gave them all my word no harm would come to them for signing this.

PARRIS. This is a clear attack upon the court!

HALE. (*To Parris. Trying to contain himself.*) Is every defense an attack upon the court? Can no one . . . ?

PARRIS. (*With pleasure.*) All innocent and Christian people are *happy* for the courts in Salem! (*Meaning people on the list.*) These people are gloomy for it —— (*To Danforth directly.*) And I think you will want to know, from each and every one of them, what discontents them with you!

HATHORNE. I think they ought to be examined, sir.

DANFORTH. It is not necessarily an attack, I think. Yet . . .

NURSE. These are all *covenanted* Christians, sir. . . .

DANFORTH. (*Kindly.*) Then I am sure they may have nothing to fear. (*Hands Cheever the paper.*) Mister Cheever, have warrants drawn for all of these—arrest for examination. (*Cheever exits* U. R. *To Proctor.*) Now, Mister, what other information do you have for us? (*Nurse is still standing, horrified.*) You may sit, Mister Nurse.

NURSE. I have brought trouble on these people, I have. . . .

DANFORTH. No, old man, you have not hurt these people if they are of good conscience. But you must understand, sir, that a person is either with this court or he must be counted against it; there be no road between. This is a sharp time, now, a precise time—we live no longer in the dusky afternoon when evil mixed itself with good and befuddled the world. Now, by God's grace, the shining sun is up, and them that fear not light will surely praise it. I hope you will be one of those. (*Mary suddenly sobs.*) She's not hearty, I see.

PROCTOR. No, she's not, sir. (*To Mary, bending to her, holding her shoulders, quietly and kindly.*) Now remember what the angel Raphael said to the boy Tobias. Remember it.

MARY. (*Hardly audible.*) Aye.

PROCTOR. "Do that which is good and no harm shall come to thee."

DANFORTH. Come, man, we wait you.

COREY. John, my deposition, give him mine.

PROCTOR. Aye. (*Cheever enters* U. R. *Proctor hands Danforth another paper.*) This is Mister Corey's deposition. (*Crosses back to above Mary, pats her shoulders, then drops hands.*)

DANFORTH. Oh? (*He looks down at it.*)

HATHORNE. (*Suspiciously.*) What lawyer drew this, Corey?

COREY. You know I never hired no lawyer in my life, Hathorne.

DANFORTH. (*Finishing the reading of it.*) It is very well-phrased. My compliments. Mister Parris, if Mr. Putnam is in the court, bring him in. (*Parris exits* D. R.) You have no legal training, Mister Corey?

COREY. I have the best, sir—I am *thirty-three* time in court in my life. And always *plaintiff*, too.

DANFORTH. (*Lightly.*) Oh, then you're much put-upon.

COREY. I am never put-upon; I know my rights, sir, and I will have them. You know, your father tried a case of mine, might be thirty-five year ago, I think.

DANFORTH. Indeed?

COREY. He never spoke to you of it?

DANFORTH. No. I cannot recall it.

COREY. That's strange. He give me nine pound damages. He were a fair judge, your father. Y'see, I had a white mare that time, and this fellow come to borrow the mare —— (*Putnam enters.*) Aye, there he is!

DANFORTH. Mr. Putnam, I have here an accusation by Mr. Corey against you. He states that you coldly prompted your daughter to cry witchery upon George Jacobs that is now in jail.

PUTNAM. It is a lie!

DANFORTH. Mr. Putnam states your charge is a lie. What say you to that?

COREY. A fart on Thomas Putnam! That is what I say to that!

DANFORTH. What proof do you submit for your charge, sir?

COREY. My proof is *there!* (*The paper.*) If Jacobs hangs for a witch he forfeit up his property—that's law! And there is none but Putnam with the coin to buy so great a piece. This man is killing his neighbors for their *land!*

DANFORTH. But proof, sir, proof. . . .

COREY. (*Emphatically.*) The proof is *there!*—I have it from an honest man who heard Putnam say it! The day his daughter cried out on Jacobs, he said she'd given him a fair gift of land.

HATHORNE. And the name of this man?

COREY. (*Taken aback.*) What name?

HATHORNE. The man that give you this information?

COREY. (*He hesitates.*) Why, I . . . I cannot give you his name.

HATHORNE. And why not?

COREY. You know well why not!—He'll lay in jail if I give his name!

HATHORNE. This is contempt of the court, Mister Danforth!

DANFORTH. (*Kindly, as to a child.*) You will surely tell us the name.

COREY. (*Quietly.*) I will not give you no name. I mentioned my wife's name once and I'll burn in hell long enough for that. I stand mute.

DANFORTH. (*Rather regretfully.*) In that case, I have no choice but to arrest you for contempt of this court, do you know that?

COREY. This is a hearing; you cannot clap me for contempt of a hearing.

DANFORTH. Oh, it is a proper lawyer! Do you wish me to

59

declare the court in full session here?—or will you give me good reply?

COREY. I cannot give you no name, sir, I cannot. . . .

DANFORTH. You are a foolish old man. Mister Cheever, *(Cheever crosses D. to stool above table. Sits, opens writing box, prepares to write. Puts on glasses.)* begin the record. The court is now in session. I ask you, Mister Corey . . .

PROCTOR. Your Honor . . . he has the story in confidence, sir, and he . . .

PARRIS. The Devil lives on such confidences! *(To Danforth.)* Without confidences there could be no conspiracy, 'Your Honor!

HATHORNE. I think it must be broken, sir.

DANFORTH. *(To Corey, in friendly tone, but a little impatient.)* Old man, if your informant tells the truth let him come here openly like a decent man. But if he hides in anonymity I must know why. Now, sir, the government and central church demand of you the name of him who reported Mister Thomas Putnam a common murderer.

HALE. *Excellency* . . .

DANFORTH. Mister Hale.

HALE. *(Regretfully.)* We cannot blink it more. There is a prodigious fear of this court in the country. . . . *(Corey nods slightly in agreement.)*

DANFORTH. Then there is a prodigious guilt in the country. Are *you* afraid to be questioned here?

HALE. *(Not sure.)* . . . I may only fear the Lord, sir, but there is fear in the country, nevertheless.

DANFORTH. *(He is angered now.)* Reproach me not with the fear in the country; there is fear in the country because there is a moving plot to topple Christ in the country!

HALE. But it does not follow that everyone accused is part of it.

DANFORTH. No uncorrupted man may fear this court, Mister Hale! *(Directly at Proctor.)* None! Mr. Corey, you are under arrest in contempt of this court. Now sit you down and take counsel with yourself, or you will be set in the jail until you decide to answer all questions.

(Corey goes for Putnam.)

PROCTOR. No, Giles!

COREY. I'll cut your throat, Putnam! I'll kill you yet.

PROCTOR. (*Put Giles on bench* L.) Peace, Giles, peace! We'll prove ourselves, now we will.

COREY. Say nothin' more, John. He's only playing you. He means to hang us all.

DANFORTH. This is a court of law, Mister. I'll have no effrontery here.

PROCTOR. Forgive him, sir, for his old age. Peace, Giles, we'll prove it all now. (*Putnam exits* D. R.)

PROCTOR. (*Crossing to* U. L. *of Mary, puts hands on her arms.*) You cannot weep, Mary. Remember the angel what he say to the boy. Hold to it, now; there is your rock. (*Mary quiets. He takes out a paper and turns to Danforth.*) This is Mary Warren's deposition. I . . . I would ask you remember, sir, while you read it, that until two week ago she were no different than the other children are today. (*He is speaking reasonably, restraining all his fears, his anger, his anxiety, like a young lawyer.*) You saw her scream, she howled, she swore familiar spirits choked her; she even testified that Satan, in the form of women now in jail, tried to win her soul away, and then when she refused . . .

DANFORTH. We know all this.

PROCTOR. Ay, sir. She swears now that she *never* saw Satan; nor *any* spirit, vague or clear, that Satan may have sent to hurt her. And she declares her friends are lying now.

HALE. Excellency, a moment. I think this goes to the heart of the matter, sir.

DANFORTH. It surely does.

HALE. I cannot say he is an honest man, I know him little. But in all justice, sir, a claim so weighty cannot be argued by a farmer. In God's name, sir, stop here; send him home and let him come again with a lawyer. . . .

DANFORTH. (*Patiently.*) Now look you, Mister Hale . . .

HALE. (*A plea of an honest man.*) Excellency, I have signed seventy-two death warrants; I am a minister of the Lord, and I dare not take a life without there be a proof so immaculate, no slightest qualm of conscience may doubt it.

DANFORTH. Mister Hale, you surely do not doubt my justice?

HALE. I have this morning signed away the soul of Rebecca Nurse, Your Honor. I'll not conceal it—I tell you true, sir, my hand shakes yet as with a wound! I pray you, sir, *this* argument let lawyers present to you.

DANFORTH. Mister Hale, believe me; for a man of such terrible learning you are most bewildered—I hope you will forgive me. (*Relishing in his knowledge of the law.*) I have been thirty-two year at the bar, sir, and I should be confounded were I called upon to defend these people. Let you consider, now—and I bid you all do likewise:—in an ordinary crime, how does one defend the accused? One calls up witnesses to prove his innocence. But witchcraft is *ipso facto*, on its face and by its nature, an invisible crime. Therefore, who may possibly be witness to it?—the witch, and the victim. None other. Now we cannot hope the witch will accuse herself; granted? Therefore, we must rely upon her victims—and they do testify, the children certainly do testify. As for the witches, none will deny that we are *most eager* for their confessions. Therefore, what is *left* for a lawyer to bring out? I think I have made my point. Have I not?

HALE. But this child claims the girls are not truthful, and if they are not . . .

DANFORTH. That is precisely what I am about to consider, sir. What more may you ask of me? Unless you doubt my probity?

HALE. (*Defeated.*) I surely do not, sir. Let you consider it, then.

DANFORTH. And let you put your heart to rest. Her deposition, Mister Proctor. (*Proctor hands it to him. Hathorne goes to L. of Danforth and starts reading. Parris comes to his side.*)

PARRIS. (*Timidly.*) I should like to question . . .

DANFORTH. (*His first real outburst, in which his contempt for Parris is clear.*) Mister Parris, I bid you be silent! Sit you down, Mr. Proctor. You sit there. (*To Mary, indicating bench D. s. of table. Proctor takes Mary to bench, returns and sits L. of table.*) Mister Cheever, will you go into the court and bring the children here. (*Cheever gets up, goes out D. R. Danforth now turns to Mary.*) Mary Warren, how came you to this turnabout? Has Mister Proctor threatened you for this deposition?

MARY. No, sir.

DANFORTH. Has he *ever* threatened you?

MARY. (*Weaker.*) No, sir.

DANFORTH. (*Sensing a weakening, harder.*) Has he threatened you?

MARY. No, sir.

DANFORTH. Then you tell me that you sat in my court, callously lying when you knew that people would hang by your evidence? Answer me!

MARY. (Almost inaudibly.) I did, sir.

DANFORTH. How were you instructed in your life?—Do you not know that God damns all liars? Or is it now that you lie?

MARY. No, sir—I am with God now.

DANFORTH. You are with God now.

MARY. Aye, sir.

DANFORTH. I will tell you this—you are either lying now, or you were lying in the court, and in either case you have committed perjury and you will go to jail for it. You cannot lightly say you lied, Mary. Do you know that?

MARY. I cannot lie no more. I am with God, I am with God. . . . (But she breaks into sobs at the thought of it. Enter Cheever, Susanna Wallcott, Mercy Lewis, and finally Abigail D R.)

CHEEVER. Ruth Putnam's not in the court, sir, nor the other children.

DANFORTH. These will be sufficient. Sit you down, children. (Silently they sit. Willard enters D. R., stands at D. R.) Your friend Mary Warren has given us a deposition. In which she swears that she never saw familiar spirits, apparitions, nor any manifest of the Devil. She claims as well, that none of you have seen these things either. Now, children, this is a court of law. The law, based upon the Bible, and the Bible writ by Almighty God, forbid the practice of witchcraft, and describe death as the penalty thereof. But, likewise, children, the law and Bible damn all liars, and bearers of false witness. Now then . . . it does not escape me that this deposition may be devised to blind us; (To Hathorne.) it may well be that Mary Warren has been conquered by Satan who sends her here to distract our sacred purpose. If so, her neck will break for it. But if she speak true, I bid you now drop your guile and confess your pretense, for a quick confession will go easier with you. Abigail Williams, rise. (Abigail rises slowly.) Is there any truth in this?

ABIGAIL. (A contemptuous look at Mary.) No, sir.

DANFORTH. Children, a very augur bit will now be turned into your souls until your honesty is proved. Will either of you change your positions now, or do you force me to hard questioning?

ABIGAIL. I have naught to change, sir. She lies.

DANFORTH. (To Mary.) You would still go on with this?

MARY. (*Faintly.*) Aye, sir.

DANFORTH. (*To Abigail.*) A poppet were discovered in Mister Proctor's house, stabbed by a needle. Mary Warren claims that you sat beside her in the court when she made it, and that you saw her make it, and witnessed how she herself stuck her needle into it for safe-keeping. What say you to that?

ABIGAIL. (*A slight note of indignation.*) It is a lie, sir. (*Mary looks at Abigail, then back* u. s.)

DANFORTH. While you worked for Mister Proctor, did you see poppets in that house?

ABIGAIL. Goody Proctor *always* kept poppets.

PROCTOR. (*Quietly.*) Your Honor, my wife never kept no poppets. Mary Warren confesses it was her poppet.

CHEEVER. Your Excellency.

DANFORTH. Mister Cheever.

CHEEVER. When I spoke with Goody Proctor in that house, she said she never kept no poppets. But she said she *did* keep poppets when she were a girl.

PROCTOR. She has not been a girl these fifteen years, your Honor.

HATHORNE. But a poppet will *keep* fifteen years, will it not?

PROCTOR. It will *keep* if it is *kept,* but Mary Warren swears she never saw no poppets in my house, nor anyone else.

PARRIS. Why could there not have been poppets hid where no one ever saw them?

PROCTOR. There might also be two golden candlesticks in my house, but no one ever saw them!

PARRIS. We are here, your Honor, precisely to discover what no one has ever seen.

PROCTOR. Mister Danforth, what profit Mary Warren to turn herself about? What may she *gain* but hard questioning and worse?

DANFORTH. (*With astonishment.*) You are charging Abigail Williams with a marvelous cool plot to murder, do you understand that?

PROCTOR. I do, sir. I believe she means to murder.

DANFORTH. (*Incredulously.*) This child would murder your wife?

PROCTOR. It is not a child, sir. Now hear me, sir. In the sight of the congregation she were twice this year put out of this meetin' house for laughter during prayer. (*Abigail bows head.*)

DANFORTH. (*Shocked, he turns to Abigail.*) What's this? Laughter during . . . !

PARRIS. Excellency . . .

DANFORTH. Do you deny it, Mister Parris?

PARRIS. I . . . do believe it happened once—she is sometimes silly, but she is solemn now.

COREY. Ay, now she is solemn and goes to hang people!

DANFORTH. Quiet, man. . . .

HATHORNE. Surely it have no bearing on the question, sir. He charges contemplation of murder.

DANFORTH. Aye. . . . (*Studying Abigail.*) But it strikes hard upon me that she will laugh at prayer. Continue, Mister Proctor.

PROCTOR. Mary.—Now tell the Governor how you danced in the woods.

PARRIS. Excellency, since I come to Salem this man is blackening my name. He . . .

DANFORTH. In a moment, sir. (*To Mary. Shocked.*) What is this dancing?

MARY. I . . . (*She glances at Abigail who is staring down at her remorselessly.*) Mister Proctor . . .

PROCTOR. Abigail leads the girls to the woods, your Honor, and they have danced there naked. . . . (*Hale crosses slowly, looks at Abigail and the girls.*)

PARRIS. Your Honor, this . . .

PROCTOR. Mister Parris discovered them there in the dead of night!—there's the "child" she is!

DANFORTH. Mister Parris . . .

PARRIS. I can only say, sir, that I never found any of them— naked, and this man is . . .

DANFORTH. You discovered them dancing in the woods? (*Eyes on Parris, he points at Abigail.*) Abigail?

HALE. Excellency, when I first arrived from Beverly, Mister Parris told me that.

DANFORTH. Do you deny it, Mister Parris?

PARRIS. I do not, sir, but I never saw any of them naked.

DANFORTH. But she have danced?

PARRIS. (*Unwillingly.*) Aye, sir.

HATHORNE. Excellency, will you permit me? (*Points at Mary.*)

DANFORTH. Pray, proceed.

HATHORNE. You say you never saw no spirits, Mary, were *never* threatened or afflicted by any manifest of the Devil or the Devil's agents?

MARY. (*Very faintly.*) No, sir.

HATHORNE. And yet, when people accused of witchery confronted you in court, you would faint, saying their spirits came out of their bodies and choked you. . . .

MARY. That were pretense, sir.

DANFORTH. I cannot hear you.

MARY. Pretense, sir.

PARRIS. But you did turn cold, did you not? I myself picked you up many times, and your skin were icy. Mister Danforth, you . . .

DANFORTH. I saw that many times.

PROCTOR. She only pretended to faint, your Excellency.— They're all marvelous pretenders.

HATHORNE. Then can she pretend to faint now?

PROCTOR. Now?

PARRIS. Why not? Now there are no spirits attacking her, for none in this room is accused of witchcraft. So let her turn herself cold now, let her pretend she is attacked now, let her faint. Faint! (*Turns to Mary.*)

MARY. Faint?

PARRIS. Aye, faint! Prove to us how you pretended in the court so many times.

MARY. (*Looks to Proctor.*) I . . . cannot faint now, sir.

PROCTOR. (*Alarmed. Quietly.*) Can you not pretend it?

MARY. I . . . I have no *sense* of it now, I . . .

DANFORTH. Why? What is lacking now?

MARY. I . . . cannot tell, sir, I . . .

DANFORTH. Might it be that here we have no afflicting spirit loose, but in the court there were some?

MARY. (*Desperately.*) I never saw no spirits.

PARRIS. Then see no spirits *now*, and prove to us that you can faint by your own will, as you claim.

MARY. (*Takes deep breath, stares searching for the emotion of it, and then shakes head.*) I . . . cannot do it.

PARRIS. Then you will confess, will you not? Attacking spirits *made* you to faint!

MARY. *No*, sir, I . . .

66

PARRIS. Your Excellency, this is a trick to blind the court.

MARY. It's not a trick! I . . . I used to faint because . . . I
. . . I *thought* I saw spirits.

DANFORTH. *Thought* you saw them!

MARY. But I did *not*, your Honor.

HATHORNE. How could you *think* you saw them *unless* you
saw them?

MARY. I . . . I cannot tell how, but I did. I . . . I heard the
other girls screaming, and *you*, your Honor, you seemed to *believe*
them and I . . . It were only *sport* in the beginning, sir, but then
the whole world cried spirits, spirits, and I . . . I promise you,
Mister Danforth, I only thought I saw them but I did not.

PARRIS. Surely your Excellency is not taken by this simple lie.

DANFORTH. (*A threat.*) Abigail Williams! (*She holds her chin
up.*) I bid you now search your heart, and tell me this—and beware of it, child, to God every soul is precious and His vengeance
is terrible on them that take life without cause. Is it possible,
child, that the spirits you have seen are illusion only, some *decep-
tion* that may cross your mind when . . .

ABIGAIL. (*Indignant.*) Why, this . . . this . . . is a base question, sir.

DANFORTH. Child, I would have you consider it ——

ABIGAIL. (*A step to him. Unafraid.*) I have been hurt, Mister
Danforth; I have seen my blood runnin' out! I have been near to
murdered every day because I done my duty pointing out the
Devil's people—and this is my reward? To be mistrusted, denied,
questioned like a . . .

DANFORTH. (*He weakens.*) Child, I do not mistrust you. . . .

ABIGAIL. (*NOW it pours. She does not wait for his speech.*)
Let *you* beware, Mister Danforth—think you to be so mighty
that the power of Hell may not turn your wits!?—beware of it!
(*She shivers and looks at Mary, then folds her arms around her.*)
—there it . . .

DANFORTH. (*Apprehensively.*) What is it, child?

ABIGAIL. (*Backing away to bench R. and sits. Clasping her arms
about her as though cold.*) I . . . I know not. A wind, a cold
wind has come. (*Her eyes fall on Mary.*)

MARY. (*Terrified, pleading.*) Abby!

MERCY. Your Honor, I freeze!

PROCTOR. They're pretending!

HATHORNE. (*Touching Abigail's hand.*) She is cold, your Honor, touch her!

MERCY. (*Rises. A threat.*) Mary, do you send this shadow on me? (*Sits slowly.*)

MARY. Lord save me! (*Susanna rises looking at Mary, then slowly sits.*)

ABIGAIL. (*She is shivering visibly.*) I freeze—I freeze. (*Mercy hugs her as they shiver.*)

MARY. (*With great fear.*) Abby, don't do that! (*Proctor crosses to her, grabs her.*)

DANFORTH. (*Himself engaged and entered by Abigail.*) Mary Warren, do you witch her? I say to you, do you send your spirit out!

MARY. (*Almost collapsing. Putting her in seat.*) Let me go, Mister Proctor, I cannot, I cannot . . .

ABIGAIL. (*Shouting.*) "Oh, Heavenly Father, take away this shadow."

PROCTOR. Whore! How do you dare call Heaven!

DANFORTH. Man! What do you ——?

PROCTOR. It is a whore.

PARRIS. Now here, here . . . !

DANFORTH. You charge ——

ABIGAIL. Mister Danforth, he's lying!

PROCTOR. Mark her, now she'll suck a scream to stab me with, but ——

DANFORTH. You will prove this, this will not pass.

PROCTOR. I have known her, sir. I have . . . known her.

DANFORTH. (*A pause. His eyes stare incredulously at Proctor.*) You . . . you are a lecher?

NURSE. (*Horrified.*) John, you cannot . . .

PROCTOR. No, Francis, it is true, it is true. (*Back to Danforth.*) She will deny it, but you will believe *me*, sir; a man . . . a man will not cast away his good name, sir, you surely know that ——

DANFORTH. In what time . . . ? In what time, in what place?

PROCTOR. (*Hanging head, turning front.*) In the proper place —where my beasts are bedded. Eight months now, sir, it is eight months. She used to serve me in my house, sir. A man may think God sleeps, but God sees everything. I know it now. I beg you, sir, I beg you—see her what she is. My wife, my dear good wife took this girl soon after, sir, and put her out on the high road.

And being what she is, a lump of vanity, sir. . . . (*Starts to weep.*) Excellency, forgive me, forgive me. She thinks to dance with me on my wife's grave! And well she might!—for I thought of her *softly;* God help me, I lusted, and there is a promise in such sweat! But it is a whore's vengeance, and you must see it; I set myself entirely in your hands, I know you must see it now. My wife is innocent, except she know a whore when she see one.

DANFORTH. (*Turns to Abigail.*) You deny every scrap and tittle of this?

ABIGAIL. (*Rising.*) If I must answer that, sir, I will leave and I will not come back again. (*Starts for D. R. exit.*)

HALE. She does not deny it, Mr. Danforth. She does not deny it!

DANFORTH. (*To Abigail.*) You will remain where you are. Sit you down! (*Looking at Abigail. Stops at U. S. of D. R. door, slowly turns to him.*) Mister Parris, go into the court and bring Goodwife Proctor out. (*Proctor crosses L. Danforth is peeved at Parris.*) Mister Parris. (*Parris stops.*) And tell her not one word of what's been spoken here. And let you knock before you enter. (*Parris goes out U. R.*) Now we shall touch the bottom of this swamp. (*To Proctor.*) Your wife, you say, is an honest woman?

PROCTOR. In her *life,* sir, she have *never lied.* There are them that cannot sing, and them that cannot weep—my wife cannot lie.

DANFORTH. And when she put this girl out of your house, she put her out for a harlot ——

PROCTOR. Ay, sir.

DANFORTH. And knew her for a harlot?

PROCTOR. She knew her for a harlot.

DANFORTH. Good, then. (*To Abigail, a threat.*) And if she tell me, child, it were for harlotry, may God spread His mercy on you! (*There is a knock at door R. He calls off.*) Hold! (*To Abigail.*) Turn your back. Turn your back. (*She does, facing D. R. To Proctor.*) You do likewise. (*Proctor faces off L.*) Now let neither of you turn to face Goody Proctor. No one in this room is to speak one word, or raise a gesture ay or nay. (*He turns toward door U. R., calls.*) Enter! (*Elizabeth enters U. R., followed by Parris. She stands alone, her eyes looking for Proctor.*) Mister Cheever, report this testimony in all exactness. Are you ready?

CHEEVER. Ready, sir.

DANFORTH. Come here, woman. (*Elizabeth crosses to R. of*

69

Danforth, looking toward Proctor.) Look at me only, not at your husband. In my eyes only. (*She looks at him.*)

ELIZABETH. Good, sir.

DANFORTH. We are given to understand that at one time you dismissed your servant, Abigail Williams.

ELIZABETH. That is true, sir.

DANFORTH. For what cause did you dismiss her? (*Elizabeth tries to glance at Proctor.*) You will look in my eyes only and not at your husband. The answer is in your memory and you need no help to give it to me. Why did you dismiss Abigail Williams?

ELIZABETH. (*Not knowing what to say, sensing a situation, she wets her lips to stall for time.*) She . . . dissatisfied me . . . (*Adding.*) and my husband.

DANFORTH. In what *way* dissatisfied you?

ELIZABETH. She were . . . (*She glances at Proctor for a cue.*)

DANFORTH. Woman, look at *me!* Were she slovenly? Lazy? What disturbance did she cause?

ELIZABETH. Your Honor, I . . . in that time I were sick. And I . . . My husband is a good and righteous man. He is never drunk, as some are, nor wastin' his time at the shovelboard, but always at his work. . . . But in my sickness—you see, sir, I were a long time sick after my last baby, and I thought I saw my husband somewhat turning from me. And this girl . . . (*She turns to Abigail.*)

DANFORTH. (*Shouting.*) Look at me!

ELIZABETH. (*Weeping.*) Aye, sir. Abigail Williams . . . (*She breaks off.*)

DANFORTH. (*Slightly impatient.*) What of Abigail Williams?

ELIZABETH. I came to think he fancied her. And so one night I lost my wits, I think, and put her out on the high road.

DANFORTH. Your husband . . . did he indeed turn from you?

ELIZABETH. (*A plea.*) My husband . . . is a goodly man, sir . . .

DANFORTH. Then he did not turn from you!

ELIZABETH. (*She starts to glance at Proctor.*) He . . .

DANFORTH. Look at me! To your own knowledge, has John Proctor ever committed the crime of lechery? (*In a crisis of indecision she cannot speak.*) Answer my question! Is your husband a lecher!

ELIZABETH. (*Faintly.*) No, sir.

DANFORTH. Remove her. (*Proctor and Abigail turn around into scene.*)

PROCTOR. Elizabeth, tell the truth, Elizabeth!

DANFORTH. She has spoken. Remove her. (*Hale crosses R. fol lowing Elizabeth.*)

PROCTOR. (*Cries out.*) Elizabeth, I have confessed it!

ELIZABETH. Oh, John! (*Goes out U. R.*)

PROCTOR. She only thought to save my name!

HALE. Excellency, it is a natural lie to tell; I beg you, stop now; before another is condemned! I may shut my conscience to it no more . . . private vengeance is working through this testimony! From the beginning this man has struck me true. I believe him now! By my oath to heaven, I believe him, and I pray you call back his wife before we . . .

DANFORTH. She spoke nothing of lechery, and this man lies!

HALE. (*He cries out in anguish.*) I believe him! I cannot turn my face from it no more. (*Pointing at Abigail.*) This girl has always struck me false! She . . . (*Abigail with a weird cry screams up to ceiling.*)

ABIGAIL. You will not! Begone! Begone, I say! (*Mercy and Susanna rise, looking up.*)

DANFORTH. What is it, child? (*But Abigail, pointing with fear, is now raising up her frightened eyes, her awed face, toward ceiling—the girls doing the same—and now Hathorne, Hale, Putnam, Cheever and Danforth do the same.*) What's there? (*He lowers his eyes from the ceiling and now he is frightened there is real tension in his voice.*) Child! (*She is transfixed—with all the girls, in complete silence, she is open-mouthed, agape at ceiling, and in great fear.*) Girls! Why do you . . . ?

MERCY. It's on the beam!—behind the rafter!

DANFORTH. (*Looking up.*) Where!

ABIGAIL. Why . . . ? Why do you come, yellow bird?

PROCTOR. (*A tone of reason, firmly.*) Where's a bird? I see no bird!

ABIGAIL. My face? My face!?

PROCTOR. Mister Hale . . .

DANFORTH. Be quiet!

PROCTOR. (*To Hale.*) . . . Do you see a bird?

DANFORTH. Be quiet!!

ABIGAIL. (*To ceiling, in a genuine conversation with the "bird,"*

71

as though trying to talk it out of attacking her.) But God made my face; you cannot want to tear my face. Envy is a deadly sin, Mary.

MARY. Abby!

ABIGAIL. (*Unperturbed, continues to "bird."*) Oh, Mary, this is a black art to change your shape. No, I cannot, I cannot stop my mouth; it's God's work I do. . . .

MARY. Abby, I'm *here!*

PROCTOR. They're pretending, Mister Danforth!

ABIGAIL. (*Now she takes a backward step, as though the bird would swoop down momentarily.*) Oh, please, Mary!—Don't come down. . . .

ANN. Her claws, she's stretching her claws!

PROCTOR. Lies—lies ——

ABIGAIL. (*Backing further, still fixed above.*) Mary, please don't hurt me!

MARY. (*To Danforth.*). I'm not hurting her!

DANFORTH. (*To Mary.*) Why does she see this vision!?

HALE. You cannot believe them.

MARY. (*Rises.*) She sees nothin'!

ABIGAIL. (*As though hypnotized, mimicking the exact tone of Mary's cry.*) She sees nothin'!

MARY. Abby, you mustn't!

ABIGAIL. (*Now all girls join, transfixed.*) Abby, you mustn't!

MARY. (*To all girls, frantically.*) I'm here, I'm here!

ABIGAIL. (*With all girls.*) I'm here, I'm here!

DANFORTH. Mary Warren!—Draw back your spirit out of them!

MARY. Mister Danforth . . . !

ABIGAIL. (*And all girls.*) Mister Danforth!

DANFORTH. Have you compacted with the Devil? Have you?

MARY. Never, never!

GIRLS. Never, never!

DANFORTH. (*Growing hysterical.*) Why can they only repeat you?!

PROCTOR. Give me a whip—I'll stop it!

MARY. They're sporting . . . !

ABIGAIL. (*And all girls, cutting her off.*) They're sporting!

MARY. (*Turning on them all, hysterically and stamping her feet.*) Abby, stop it!

72

ABIGAIL. (*And all girls, stamping their feet.*) Abby, stop it!

MARY. (*Screaming it out at top of her lungs, and raising her fists.*) Stop it!!

ABIGAIL. (*And all, raising their fists.*) Stop it!!

MARY. Stop it.

GIRLS. Stop it.

(*Mary, utterly confounded, and becoming overwhelmed by Abigail —and the girls'—utter conviction, starts to whimper, hands half raised, powerless—and all girls begin whimpering exactly as she does.*)

DANFORTH. A little while ago you were afflicted. Now it seems you afflict others; where did you find this power?

MARY. (*Staring at Abigail.*) I . . . have no power.

ABILGAIL and ALL GIRLS. I have no power.

PROCTOR. They're gulling you, Mister!

DANFORTH. Why did you turn about this past two weeks? You have seen the Devil, have you not?

MARY. I . . .

GIRLS. I . . .

PROCTOR. (*Sensing her weakening.*) Mary, Mary, God damns all liars!

DANFORTH. (*Pounding it into her.*) You have seen the Devil, you have made compact with Lucifer, have you not?

PROCTOR. (*Quietly.*) God damns liars, Mary! (*Mary utters something unintelligible, staring at Abigail who keeps watching the "bird" above.*)

DANFORTH. I cannot hear you. What do you say? (*Mary utters again unintelligibly.*) You will confess yourself or you will hang! (*He turns her roughly to face him.*) Do you know who I am? I say you will hang if you do not open with me!

PROCTOR. Mary, remember the angel Raphael . . . do that which is good and ,

ABIGAIL. (*Pointing upward.*) The wings! Her wings are spreading! Mary, please, don't, don't . . . ! She's going to come down! She's walking the beam! Look out! *She's coming down!* (*All scream. Abigail dashes across stage as though pursued; the other girls streak hysterically in and out between the men, all converging D. S. R.—and as their screaming subsides only Mary Warren's is left, All watch her, struck, even horrified by this evident fit.*)

PROCTOR. (*Leaning across the table, turning her gently by the arm.*) Mary, tell the Governor what they . . .

MARY. (*Backing away.*) Don't touch me . . . don't touch me!

PROCTOR. Mary!

MARY. (*Pointing at Proctor.*) You are the Devil's man!

PARRIS. Praise God!

PROCTOR. Mary, how . . . ?

MARY. I'll not hang with you! I love God, I love God ——

DANFORTH. (*To Mary.*) He bid you do the Devil's work?

MARY. (*Hysterically, indicating Proctor.*) He come at me by night and every day to sign, to sign, to . . .

DANFORTH. Sign what?

PARRIS. The Devil's book? He come with a book?

MARY. (*Hysterically, pointing at Proctor.*) My name, he want my name; I'll murder you, he says, if my wife hangs! We must go and overthrow the court, he says . . . !

PROCTOR. (*Eyes follow Mary.*) Mister Hale . . . !

MARY. (*Her sobs beginning.*) He wake me every night, his eyes were like coals and his fingers claw my neck, and I sign, I sign. . . .

HALE. Excellency, the child's gone wild.

PROCTOR. Mary, Mary . . . !

MARY. (*Screaming at him.*) No, I love God; I go your way no more, (*Looking at Abigail.*) I love God, I bless God. . . . (*Sobbing, she rushes to Abigail.*) Abby, Abby, I'll never hurt you more! (*All watch, as Abigail reaches out and draws sobbing Mary to her, then looks up to Danforth.*)

DANFORTH. What are you! You are combined with anti-Christ, are you not? I have seen your power, Mister, you will not deny it!

HALE. This is not witchcraft! These girls are frauds! You condemn an honest man!

DANFORTH. I will have nothing from you, Mister Hale! (*To Proctor.*) Will you confess yourself befouled with hell, or do you keep that black allegiance yet? What say you?

PROCTOR. I say . . . God is dead!

PARRIS. (*Crossing l. toward door.*) Hear it, hear it!

PROCTOR. A fire, a fire is burning! I hear the boot of Lucifer, I see his filthy face. And it is my face and yours, Danforth. For them that quail to bring men out of ignorance, as I have quailed, and as you quail now when you know in all your black hearts that this be fraud. God damns our kind especially, and we will burn, we will burn together!

DANFORTH. Marshal, take him and Corey with him to the jail!

HALE. (*Crossing* D. L.) I denounce these proceedings! I quit this court! (*Hale exits* D. L.)

PROCTOR. You are pulling heaven down and raising up a whore.

DANFORTH. (*Shocked.*) Mister Hale, Mister Hale!

CURTAIN

ACT II

SCENE 3

Three months later. A cell in Salem jail.

A high barred window at back L., *a door upstage* R. *Two benches down stage* L. *and* R. *Stool* U. R. *of* L. *bench. The barred window effect was achieved in the Broadway production by making a "gobo" of small laths nailed across each other, leaving approximately two inch square openings. If this is put in front of the light supplying light for sunlight and moonlight effects, a bar-like effect is produced on the floor and faces of the actors who stand in the beam. There is only one entrance to this scene. In the Broadway production it was* U. R. *The night sky is seen through the window, and moonlight pouring through. The cell is otherwise in darkness, cold shadows blackening it.*

On the rise, the place appears empty. Off in the distance the painful bellowing of a cow is heard, crying to be milked. Tituba lying on R. *bench. Sarah lying bench* L. *Willard enters with two lanterns, drinks from flask which he carries.*)

WILLARD. (*Crossing* L. *toward bench.*) Sarah, wake up! Sarah Good! (*Crosses* R. *to Tituba, shakes her.*) Tituba.

SARAH. (*Sits up.*) Oh, majesty! Comin', comin'! (*Uncovering herself.*) Tituba, he's here! His Majesty's come! (*Untangling rags from legs and feet.*)

75

WILLARD. (*At window* U. L.) Go to the north cell, this place is wanted now.

TITUBA. That don't look to me like His Majesty; look to me like the Marshal. (*Slowly sits up, yawning.*)

WILLARD. (*Takes out flask.*) Get along with you now, clear this place. (*He drinks.*)

SARAH. (*Scratching herself.*) Oh, is it you, Marshal? I thought sure you be the Devil comin' for us. . . . Could I have a sip of cider for me goin'-away?

WILLARD. (*Handing her flask.*) And where are you off to, Sarah? (*Tituba untangling rags.*)

TITUBA. (*As Sarah drinks.*) We goin' to Barbados, soon the Devil gits here with the feathers and the wings.

WILLARD. Oh? A happy voyage to you.

SARAH. A pair of bluebirds wingin' southerly, the two of us!— Oh, it be a grand transformation, Marshal! (*She raises the flask to drink again.*)

WILLARD. (*Taking flask from her.*) You'd best give me that or you'll never rise off the ground. Come along now. (*Tituba rises, picks up her rags.*)

TITUBA. I'll speak to him for you, if you desire to come along, Marshal.

WILLARD. I'd not refuse it, Tituba; it is the proper morning to fly into Hell. (*Sarah folding rags.*)

TITUBA. (*Folding rags that covered her.*) Oh, it ain't no Hell in Barbados. Devil, him be pleasure-man in Barbados, him be singin' and dancin' in Barbados. You folks, you riles him up 'round here; it be too cold 'round here for that Old Boy. He freeze his soul in Massachusetts, but in Barbados, he just as sweet and —— (*Sarah rises with bundle. A bellowing cow is heard, and Tituba leaps up and calls to off.*) Yes, sir! That's him, Sarah!

SARAH. (*Toward window.*) I'm here, Majesty. (*Hopkins enters.*)

HOPKINS. The Deputy-Governor's arrived.

WILLARD. Come along, come along. . . .

TITUBA. No, he comin' for me. . . . I goin' home!

WILLARD. (*Crossing* D., *taking Tituba's* R. *arm, takes few steps as Sarah crosses to them, takes her* L. *arm. Pulling her to door* R.) That ain't Satan, just a poor old cow with a hatful of milk. Come along now, out with you.

76

TITUBA. (*Calling toward window.*) Take me home, Devil! Take me home!

SARAH. (*Following Tituba out* D. *hallway to off* L.) Tell him I'm goin', Tituba! Now you tell him Sarah Good is goin', too! (*Off stage Tituba calls on—"Take me home, Devil, Devil, take me home!" And Hopkins' voice ordering her to move on. Then Willard returns, crosses* D. L. *and clears straw from* L. *bench. Enter Danforth and Judge Hathorne. They are in greatcoats and wear hats. They are followed in by Cheever, who carries a dispatch case and a flat wooden box containing his writing materials. Cheever crosses slowly near window.*)

WILLARD. (*At bench* L.) Good morning, Majesty.

DANFORTH. Where is Mister Parris?

WILLARD. I'll fetch him.

DANFORTH. Marshal. When did Reverend Hale arrive?

WILLARD. It were toward midnight, I think.

DANFORTH. (*Suspiciously.*) What is he about here?

WILLARD. He goes among them that will hang, sir. And he prays with them. He sits with Goody Nurse now. (*Crossing to* R. *bench, clears straw from it.*) And Mister Parris with him.

DANFORTH. Indeed. That man have no authority to enter here, Marshal; why have you let him in? (*Hathorne sits bench* L.)

WILLARD. (*Laughing.*) Why, Mister Parris command me, sir. I cannot deny him.

DANFORTH. Are you drunk, Marshal?

WILLARD. No, sir, it is a bitter night, and I have no fire here.

DANFORTH. Fetch Mister Parris.

WILLARD. (*Crossing toward entrance.*) Aye, sir.

DANFORTH. There is a prodigious *stench* in this place.

WILLARD. (*Stopping at door.*) I have only now cleared the people out for you.

DANFORTH. Beware hard drink, Marshal.

WILLARD. Ay, sir. (*Exits.*)

HATHORNE. Let you question Hale, Excellency; I should not be surprised he have been preachin' in Andover lately.

DANFORTH. We'll come to that; speak nothin' of Andover. Parris prays with him. That's strange. (*Blows on his hands.*)

HATHORNE. I think sometimes Parris has a mad look these days.

DANFORTH. Mad?

HATHORNE. I met him yesterday coming out of his house, and

I bid him good morning—and he wept, and went his way. I think it is not well the village sees him so unsteady.

DANFORTH. Perhaps he have some sorrow.

CHEEVER. I think it be the *cows*, sir.

DANFORTH. The cows?

CHEEVER. There be so many *cows* wanderin' the highroads, now their masters are in the jails, and much disagreement who they will belong to now. I know Mister Parris be arguin' with farmers all yesterday—there is great contention, sir, about the cows. (*Danforth sits bench* R.) Contention make him weep, sir, it were always a man that weep for contention. (*He turns, as do Hathorne and Danforth, hearing a man coming up the corridor off* U. R. *Danforth raises his head as Parris enters. He is gaunt, frightened and sweating.*)

PARRIS. (*To Danforth, instantly.*) Oh, good morning, sir, thank you for comin', I beg your pardon wakin' you so early. Good morning, Judge Hathorne. . . .

DANFORTH. Reverend Hale have no right to enter this . . .

PARRIS. Excellency, a moment.

HATHORNE. Do you leave him alone with the prisoners?

DANFORTH. What's his business here?

PARRIS. (*Prayerfully holding up his hands.*) Excellency, hear me. It is a providence. Reverend Hale has returned to bring Rebecca Nurse to God.

DANFORTH. He bids her confess?

PARRIS. (*Sitting.*) Hear me. (*Cheever crosses, sits end of* L. *bench.*) Rebecca have not given me a word this three month since she came. Now she sits with him, and her sister and Martha Corey and two or three others, and he pleads with them confess their crimes and save their lives.

DANFORTH. Why—this is indeed a providence. And they soften, they soften?

PARRIS. Not yet, not yet. But I thought to summon you, sir, that we might think on whether it be not wise to . . . there is news, sir, that the court, the court must reckon with. My niece . . . I believe she has vanished.

DANFORTH. Vanished! (*Hathorne rises.*)

PARRIS. I had thought to advise you of it earlier in the week, but . . .

DANFORTH. Why?—how long is she gone?

PARRIS. This be the third night—Mercy Lewis is gone, too.

DANFORTH. (*Alarmed.*) I will send a party for them. Where may they be?

PARRIS. Excellency, I think they be aboard a ship. My daughter tells me now she heard them speakin' of ships last week, and tonight I discover my . . . my strongbox is broke into.

HATHORNE. (*Astonished.*) She have robbed you?!

PARRIS. Thirty-one pound is gone. I am penniless.

DANFORTH. (*Rising.*) Mister Parris, you are a brainless man!

PARRIS. Excellency, it profit nothing you should blame me. I cannot think they would run off except they fear to keep in Salem any more—since the news of Andover has broken here. . . .

DANFORTH. Andover is remedied. The court returns there on Friday, and will resume examinations.

PARRIS. I am sure of it, sir. But the rumor here speaks rebellion in Andover, and it . . .

DANFORTH. (*Strongly protesting.*) There is no rebellion in Andover.

PARRIS. I tell you what is said here, sir. Andover have thrown out the *court*, they say, and will have no part of witchcraft. There be a faction here feeding on that news, and I tell you true, sir, I fear there will be riot here.

HATHORNE. Riot!—Why, at every execution I have seen naught but high satisfaction in the town. (*Danforth sits bench* L.)

PARRIS. Judge Hathorne—it were another sort that hanged till now. Rebecca Nurse is no Bridget that lived three year with Bishop before she married him. John Proctor is not Isaac Ward that drank his family to ruin. (*To Danforth.*) Let Rebecca stand upon the gibbet and send up some righteous prayer, and I fear she'll wake a vengeance on you.

HATHORNE. Excellency, she is condemned a witch. The court have . . .

DANFORTH. (*In deep concern he raises a hand to Hathorne.*) Pray you. (*To Parris.*) How do you propose, then?

PARRIS. Excellency . . . I would postpone these hangin's for a time.

DANFORTH. There will be no postponement.

PARRIS. Now Mister Hale's returned, there is hope, I think— for if he bring even *one* of these to God, that confession surely *damns* the *others* in the public eye, and none may doubt more

79

that they are all linked to Hell. This way, unconfessed and claiming innocence, doubts are *multiplied,* many honest people will weep for them, and our good purpose is *lost* in their tears.

DANFORTH. Cheever, give me the list. (*Cheever opens dispatch case, searches.*)

PARRIS. It cannot be forgot, sir, (*Danforth rises, gets list from Cheever, takes spectacles out and reads by light of lamp.*) that when I summoned the congregation for John Proctor's excommunication, there were hardly thirty people come to hear it. That speak a discontent, I think, and . . .

DANFORTH. There will be no postponement.

PARRIS. Excellency . . .

DANFORTH. Now, sir—which of these in your opinion may be brought to God? I will myself strive with him till dawn. (*Crosses to Cheever, hands him list.*)

PARRIS. There is not sufficient time till dawn. . . .

DANFORTH. I shall do my utmost. Which of them do you have hope for?

PARRIS. (*In a quavering voice, quietly.*) Excellency . . . a dagger . . . (*He chokes up.*)

DANFORTH. (*Irritated.*) What do you say?

PARRIS. Tonight, when I open my door to leave my house—a dagger clattered to the ground. (*Pleading plaintively.*) You cannot hang this sort. There is danger for *me.* I dare not step outside at night. (*Hale enters. They look at him for an instant in silence. He is steeped in sorrow, exhausted, and more direct than he ever was.*)

DANFORTH. Accept my congratulations, Reverend Hale; we are gladdened to see you returned to your good work.

HALE. You must pardon them. They will not budge.

DANFORTH. You misunderstand, sir; I cannot pardon these when twelve are already hanged for the same crime. It is not just.

PARRIS. Rebecca will not confess?

HALE. The sun will rise in a few minutes. Excellency, I must have more time.

DANFORTH. Now hear me, and beguile yourselves no more. I will not receive a single plea for pardon or postponement. Them that will not confess will hang. Twelve are already executed; the names of these seven are given out, and the village expects to see them die at dawn. Postponement, now, speaks a . . . a floundering

(*Willard enters.*) on my part; reprieve or pardon must cast doubt upon the guilt of them that died till now. While I speak God's law, I will not crack its voice with whimpering. If retaliation is your fear, know this—I should hang ten thousand that dared to rise against the law, and an ocean of salt tears could not melt the resolution of the statutes. Now draw yourselves up like men and help me, as you are bound by heaven to do.—Have you spoken with them all, Mister Hale?

HALE. All but Proctor. He is in the dungeon.

DANFORTH. (*To Hathorne.*) What's Proctor's way now? (*Hale sits bench* R.)

WILLARD. (*In doorway. Drunkenly.*) He sits like some great bird; you'd not know he lived except he will take food from time to time.

DANFORTH. (*Thinks.*) His wife . . . his wife must be well on with child now.

WILLARD. She is, sir.

DANFORTH. What think you, Mister Parris?—You have closer knowledge of this man; might her presence soften him?

PARRIS. It is possible, sir—he have not laid eyes on her these three months. I should summon her.

DANFORTH. (*To Willard.*) Is he yet adamant?—Has he struck at you again?

WILLARD. (*Smiling drunkenly.*) He cannot, sir, he is chained to the wall now.

DANFORTH. Fetch Goody Proctor to me. Then let you bring him up. (*Sits bench* U. S. *of Parris.*)

WILLARD. Ay, sir. (*Willard goes out. Silence.*)

HALE. Excellency, if you postpone a week, and publish to the town that you are striving for their confessions, that speak *mercy* on your part, not *faltering*.

DANFORTH. Mister Hale, as God have not empowered me like Joshua to stop this sun from rising, so I cannot withhold from them the perfection of their punishment.

HALE. (*Rising, crossing up to door.*) If you think God wills you to raise rebellion, Mister Danforth, you are mistaken.

DANFORTH. You have heard rebellion spoken in Salem?

HALE. Excellency, there are orphans wandering from house to house; abandoned cattle bellow on the highroads, the stink of rotting crops hangs everywhere, and no man knows when the harlots' cry will end his life—and you wonder yet if rebellion's spoke? Better you should marvel how they do not burn your province!

DANFORTH. Mister Hale, have you preached in Andover this month?

HALE. Thank God they have no need of me in Andover.

DANFORTH. You baffle me, sir. Why have you returned here?

HALE. Why, it is all simple. I come to do the Devil's work. I come to counsel Christians they should belie themselves. There is blood on my head! Can you not see the blood on my head!!

PARRIS. Hush! (*All face entrance. Willard and Elizabeth enter. Willard goes out again.*)

DANFORTH. (*Very politely.*) Goody Proctor. I hope you are hearty?

ELIZABETH. I am yet six month before my time.

DANFORTH. Pray, be at your ease, we come not for your life. We . . . (*Uncertain how to plead, for he is not accustomed to it.*) Mister Hale, will you speak with the woman?

HALE. Goody Proctor, your husband is marked to hang this morning.

ELIZABETH. (*Quietly.*) I have heard it.

HALE. (*He finds it difficult to look at her.*) You know, do you not, that I have no connection with the court? I come of my own, Goody Proctor. (*She knows this to be untrue.*) I would save your husband's life, for if he is taken I count myself his murderer. Do you understand me?

ELIZABETH. What do you want of me?

HALE. Goody Proctor . . . I have gone this three month like our Lord into the wilderness. I have sought a Christian way, for damnation's doubled on a minister who counsels men to lie.

HATHORNE. It is no lie, you cannot speak of lies. . . .

HALE. It is a lie!—they are innocent!

DANFORTH. No more. No more. I'll hear no more of that.

HALE. (*To Elizabeth.*) Let you not mistake your duty as I mistook my own. I came into this village like a bridegroom to his beloved; bearing gifts of high religion, the very crowns of holy law I brought, and what I touched with my bright confidence, it died; and where I turned the eye of my great faith, blood flowed up. Beware, Goody Proctor—cleave to no faith when faith brings blood. It is mistaken law that leads you to sacrifice. (*She looks at *him then front.*) Life, woman, life is God's most precious gift; no principle however glorious may justify the taking of it. I beg you, woman—prevail upon your husband to confess. Let him give his lie. Quail not before God's judgment in this, for it may well be God damns a liar less than he that throws his life away for pride. Will you plead with him? I cannot think he will listen to another. ELIZABETH. (*Quietly. With loathing.*) I think that be the Devil's argument.

HALE. Woman, before the laws of God we are as swine. We cannot read His will.

ELIZABETH. (*Sincerely—simply.*) I cannot dispute with you, sir, I lack learning for it.

DANFORTH. (*Irritated.*) Goody Proctor, you are not summoned here for disputation—be there no wifely tenderness within you? He will die with the sunrise. Your husband. Do you understand it? What say you? Will you contend with him? (*She is silent, staring at him.*) Are you stone? I tell you true, woman, had I no other proof of your unnatural life, your dry eyes now would be sufficient evidence that you delivered up your soul to Hell!—a very ape would weep at such calamity! Have the devil dried up any tear of pity in you? (*She is silent.*) Take her out—it profit nothing she should speak to him!

ELIZABETH. (*Quietly.*) Let me speak with him, Excellency.

PARRIS. (*With hope.*) You'll strive with him? (*She hesitates.*)

DANFORTH. Will you plead for his confession, or will you not!

ELIZABETH. I promise nothing. Let me speak with him. (*A sound—the sibilance of dragging feet on stone. They turn. Pause. Willard enters with Proctor. His wrists are chained. Willard removes them and exits. He is another man, bearded, filthy, his eyes misty as webs had overgrown them. Halts inside doorway, his eye caught by the sight of Elizabeth. The emotion flowing between them prevents anyone from speaking for an instant. Hale looks up stage. Proctor crosses down slowly toward Elizabeth, looks around, then Hale speaks.*)

HALE. Pray, leave them, Excellency. (*Exits.*)

DANFORTH. (*Parris and Cheever rise.*) Mister Proctor, you have been notified, have you not?—(*Proctor is silent, staring at Elizabeth.*) I see light in the sky, Mister; let you counsel with your wife and may God help you turn your back on hell. (*Proctor*

*is silent, staring at Elizabeth. Danforth exits. Cheever follows,
then Hathorne.)*

PARRIS. If you desire a cup of cider, Mister Proctor, I am sure
I . . . *(Proctor turns an icy stare at him and he breaks off.
Parris raises his palms toward him.)* God lead you now. *(Parris
goes out. It is as though Elizabeth and Proctor stood in a spinning
world. It is beyond sorrow, above it. They move together, clasp
hands.)*

ELIZABETH. You have been chained?

PROCTOR. *(Feeling his wrists.)* Aye. The child?

ELIZABETH. It grows.

PROCTOR. There is no word of the boys?

ELIZABETH. They're well. Rebecca's Daniel keeps them.

PROCTOR. You have not seen them?

ELIZABETH. I have not. . . .

PROCTOR. You are a . . . marvel, Elizabeth. They come for my
life now.

ELIZABETH. I know it.

PROCTOR. None . . . have yet confessed?

ELIZABETH. There be many confessed.

PROCTOR. Who are they?

ELIZABETH. There be a hundred or more, they say. Goody
Ballard is one; *(He turns his head away.)* Isaiah Goodkind, is
one. . . . There be many.

PROCTOR. Rebecca . . . ?

ELIZABETH. Not Rebecca. *(He smiles slightly in admiration,
nodding. She then speaks.)* She is one foot in heaven now. Naught
may hurt her more.

PROCTOR. *(Looking at her.)* And Giles?

ELIZABETH. You have not heard of it?

PROCTOR. I hear nothin', where I am kept.

ELIZABETH. Giles is dead.

PROCTOR. *(He looks at her incredulously.)* When were he
hanged?

ELIZABETH. *(Quietly, factually.)* He were not hanged. He would
not answer ay or nay to his indictment; for if he denied the
charge they'd hang him surely, and auction out his property. So
he stand mute, and died Christian under the law. *(He nods.)* And
so his sons will have his farm. It is the law, for he could not be
condemned a wizard without he answer the indictment, ay or nay.

PROCTOR. (*Not looking at her.*) Then how does he die?

ELIZABETH. (*Gently.*) . . . They press him, John.

PROCTOR. (*Looking at her.*) Press?

ELIZABETH. Great stones they lay upon his chest until he plead ay or nay. (*With a tender smile for the old man.*) They say he give them but two words. "More weight," he says. And died.

PROCTOR. (*Nodding, smiling grimly in admiration.*) More weight!

ELIZABETH. Ay. It were a fearsome man, Giles Corey. (*Pause.*)

PROCTOR. (*With a shy smile. Elizabeth crossing to D. S. end of bench, sits.*) I have been thinkin' I would confess to them. (*She shows nothing.*) What say you?—if I give them that?

ELIZABETH. I cannot judge you, John.

PROCTOR. (*Taking her R. hand with his L. hand, pulls her down to bench, not looking at her.*) What would you have me do?

ELIZABETH. As you will, I would have it. (*Slight pause.*) I want you living, John. That's sure.

PROCTOR. (*Hopefully.*) Giles' wife?—have she confessed?

ELIZABETH. (*Shaking her head.*) She will not.

PROCTOR. (*Taking his hand away from her.*) It is a pretense, Elizabeth.

ELIZABETH. What is?

PROCTOR. (*Trying to convince himself.*) I cannot mount the gibbet like a saint. It is a fraud. I am not that man. (*She is silent.*) My honesty is broke, Elizabeth, I am no good man. Nothing's spoiled by giving them this lie that were not rotten long before.

ELIZABETH. And yet you've not confessed till now. That speak goodness in you.

PROCTOR. (*Bitterly smiling.*) Spite. Spite only keeps me silent. It is hard to give a lie to dogs! (*He takes her R. hand, holds it.*) I would have your forgiveness, Elizabeth.

ELIZABETH. It is not for me to give, John, I am . . .

PROCTOR. I would have you see some honesty in it. Let them that never lied die now to keep their souls. It is pretense for me, a vanity that will not blind God nor keep my children out of the wind. What say you?

ELIZABETH. John . . . it come to naught that I should forgive you. Will you forgive yourself? It is your soul, John. (*He bows his head.*) Only be sure of this, for I know it now: Whatever you will do, it is a good man does it. I have read my heart this three

85

month, John. I have sins of my own to count. It needs a cold wife to prompt lechery. . . .

PROCTOR. (*In great pain.*) Enough, enough. . . .

ELIZABETH. Better you should know me!

PROCTOR. (*Turning away.*) I will not hear it!—I know you!

ELIZABETH. (*Trying to turn him back, taking his hands.*) You take my sins upon you, John!

PROCTOR. (*In agony.*) No, I take my own, my own!

ELIZABETH. (*She gropes for the words to express her feeling.*) I counted myself so plain, so poorly-made, no honest love could come to me! Suspicion kissed you when I did; I never knew how I should say my love. It were a cold house I kept . . . ! (*Hathorne enters.*)

HATHORNE. What say you, Proctor? The sun is soon up. (*Proctor lifts his head.*)

ELIZABETH. (*Warmly.*) Do what you will. But let none be your judge, there be no higher judge under heaven than Proctor is! Forgive me, forgive me, John—I never knew such goodness in the world!

PROCTOR. I want my life.

HATHORNE. You'll confess yourself?!

PROCTOR. I will have my life.

HATHORNE. God be praised!—It is a providence! (*Hathorne rushes out door, his voice is heard calling offstage.*) He will confess! Proctor will confess!

PROCTOR. (*With a cry. Rising.*) Why do you cry it! It is evil, is it not? It is *evil.*

ELIZABETH. (*Weeping.*) I cannot judge you, John, I cannot!

PROCTOR. Then who will judge me? (*Suddenly clasping his hands.*) God in Heaven, what is John Proctor, what is John Proctor! (*A fury is riding in him, a tantalized search.*) I think it is honest, I think so: I am no *saint.* Let Rebecca go like a saint, for me it is *fraud!*

ELIZABETH. I am not your judge, I cannot be . . .

PROCTOR. Would you give them such a lie? Say it. Would you ever give them this? (*She can't answer.*) You would not; if tongs of fire were singeing you you would not!—it is *evil.* (*Slight pause. Sitting.*) Good then, it is *evil,* and I *do* it! (*Hathorne enters with Danforth, and with them Cheever, Parris and Hale. It is a business-like, rapid entrance, as though the ice had been broken.*)

86

DANFORTH. Praise to God, man, praise to God; you shall be blessed in Heaven for this. (*Cheever hurries to u. s. end of bench, puts writing box on stool, prepares to write. Proctor watches him.*) Now then . . . let us have it. Are you ready, Mister Cheever?

PROCTOR. Why must it be written?

DANFORTH. Why, for the good instruction of the village, Mister; this we shall post upon the church door! (*To Parris, urgently.*) Where is the Marshal?

PARRIS. (*Runs to entrance, calls, then returns to door.*) Willard! Hurry! (*We hear Willard running off.*)

DANFORTH. Now, then, Mister, will you speak slowly, and directly to the point for Mister Cheever's sake? (*He is dictating to Cheever, who writes.*) Mister Proctor, have you seen the Devil in your life? (*Proctor's jaws lock.*) Come, man, there is light in the sky; the town waits at the scaffold; I would give out this news. Did you see the Devil?

PROCTOR. (*Looks at him, then away, and speaks.*) I did.

PARRIS. Praise God!

DANFORTH. And when he come to you, what were his demand? Did he bid you to do his work upon the earth?

PROCTOR. He did.

DANFORTH. (*Starting ʀ.*) And you bound yourself to his service? (*Danforth turns, as Rebecca and Willard enter.*) Ah, Rebecca Nurse.—Come in, come in, woman! (*Willard stays at entrance.*)

REBECCA. (*Seeing him she brightens.*) Ah, John! You are well, then, eh?

DANFORTH. Courage, man, courage—let her witness your good example that she may come to God herself. Now hear it, Goody Nurse! Say on, Mister Proctor—did you bind yourself to the Devil's service?

REBECCA. Why, John!

PROCTOR. (*Face turned from Rebecca.*) I did.

DANFORTH. Now, woman, you surely see it profit nothin' to keep this conspiracy any further. Will you confess yourself with him?

REBECCA. Oh, John—God send His mercy on you!

PROCTOR. Take her out!

DANFORTH. I say will you confess yourself, Goody Nurse!

REBECCA. Why, it is a lie, it is a lie; how may I damn myself? I cannot, I cannot. (*Proctor turns away.*)

DANFORTH. Mister Proctor. When the Devil came to you did you see Rebecca Nurse in his company? Come, man, take courage —did you ever see her with the Devil?

PROCTOR. (*Almost inaudibly, in agony.*) No. (*Rebecca takes a step toward him.*)

DANFORTH. Did you ever see her sister, Mary Easty, with the Devil?

PROCTOR. No, I did not.

DANFORTH. Did you ever see (*Proctor rises, crosses toward* R. *aware of Rebecca looking at him, hurries past her.*) Martha Corey with the Devil?

PROCTOR. I did not.

DANFORTH. Did you ever see anyone with the Devil?

PROCTOR. I did not. (*Sitting bench* R.)

DANFORTH. Proctor—you mistake me. I am not empowered to trade your life for a lie. You have most certainly seen some person with the Devil. (*Proctor is silent.*) Mister Proctor, a score of people have already testified they saw this woman with the Devil. . . .

PROCTOR. Then it is *proved.* Why must I *say* it?

DANFORTH. Why "must" you say it! Why, you should rejoice to say it if your soul is purged of any love for Hell!

PROCTOR. They think to go like saints. I like not to spoil their names.

DANFORTH. Mister Proctor, do you think they go like saints? Look you, sir—I think you mistake your duty here. It matters nothing what she thought—she is convicted of the unnatural murder of children, and you for sending your spirit out upon Mary Warren. Your soul alone is the issue here, Mister, and you will prove its whiteness or you cannot live in a Christian country. Will you tell me now what persons conspired with you in the Devil's company? To your knowledge was Rebecca Nurse ever . . . ?

PROCTOR. I speak my own sins, I cannot judge another. I have no tongue for it.

HALE. Excellency, it is enough he confess himself. Let him sign it, let him sign it. . . .

PARRIS. It is a great service, sir—it is a weighty name, it will strike the village that he confess. I beg you, let him sign it. The sun is up, Excellency!

DANFORTH. (*To Proctor.*) Come then, sign your testimony. Mr. Cheever, take it to him. (*Cheever gives Proctor a pen.*) Come, man, sign it.

PROCTOR. You have all witnessed it—it is enough.

DANFORTH. You will not sign it?!

PROCTOR. (*Desperately.*) You have all witnessed it; what more is needed?

DANFORTH. Do you sport with me? You will sign your name or it is no confession, Mister! (*Proctor signs.*) Your second name, man. (*Proctor signs last name.*)

PARRIS. Praise be to the Lord!

DANFORTH. (*Perplexed, but politely extending his hand.*) If you please, sir.

PROCTOR. (*Dumbly, looking at paper.*) No.

DANFORTH. Mister Proctor, I must have . . .

PROCTOR. (*Putting paper behind him. Childishly befuddled.*) No—no. I have signed it. You have seen me. It is done! You have no need for this.

PARRIS. Proctor, the village must have proof that . . .

PROCTOR. Damn the village! I confess to God and God has seen my name on this! It is *enough!*

DANFORTH. No, sir, it is . . .

PROCTOR. You came to save my soul, did you not? Here!—I have confessed myself, it is enough!

DANFORTH. You have not con . . .

PROCTOR. I have confessed myself! Is there no good penitence but it be public? God does not need my name nailed upon the church! God sees my name, God knows how black my sins are!—it is enough!

DANFORTH. Mister Proctor .

PROCTOR. You will not use me! I am no Sarah Good or Tituba, I am John Proctor! You will not use me! It is no part of salvation that you should use me!

DANFORTH. I do not wish to . . .

PROCTOR. I have three children—how may I teach them to walk like men in the world and I sold my friends?!

DANFORTH. You have not sold your friends. . . .

PROCTOR. Beguile me not!—I blacken all of them when this is nailed to the church the very day they hang for silence!

DANFORTH. Mister Proctor, I must have good and legal proof that you . . .

PROCTOR. You are the high court, your word is good enough! Tell them I confessed myself; say Proctor broke his knees and wept like a woman; say what you will, but my name cannot . . .

DANFORTH. (*With suspicion.*) It is the same, is it not?—if I report it or you sign to it?

PROCTOR. (*He knows it is childish.*) No, it is not the same! What others say and what I sign to is not the same!

DANFORTH. Why? Do you mean to deny this confession when you are free?

PROCTOR. (*Rising.*) I mean to deny nothing!

DANFORTH. Then explain to me, Mr. Proctor, why you will not let . . .

PROCTOR. Because it is my *name!* Because I cannot have another in my life! Because I *lie* and sign myself to lies! Because I am not worth the dust on the feet of them that hang! How may I live without my name? I have given you my soul, leave me my name!

DANFORTH. (*Pointing at confession in Proctor's hand.*) Is that document a lie? If it is a lie I will not accept it! What say you? I will not deal in lies, Mister! (*During this speech Proctor looks at Danforth, then Rebecca, then Elizabeth.*) You will give me your honest confession in my hand, or I cannot keep you from the rope. What way do you go, Mister? (*Proctor deliberately tears paper once.*) Marshal. (*Willard comes from entrance to inside room.*)

PARRIS. Proctor, Proctor!

HALE. Man, you will hang!—You cannot!

PROCTOR. (*Crossing slowly R. to Elizabeth, takes her hands for a moment. Simply, with dignity.*) Pray God it speak some goodness for me. (*They embrace. He then holds her at arm's length.*) Give them no tear. Show them a heart of stone and sink them with it.

REBECCA. Let you fear nothing. There is another judgment waits us all.

DANFORTH. (*To Willard.*) Hang them high over the town. Whoever weeps (*Crossing up toward door.*) for these weeps for corruption. Take them! (*Proctor crosses to* L. *of Rebecca. Danforth exits. Hathorne also exits. Rebecca starts for door. Proctor takes her arm.*)

WILLARD. Come, man. (*Crossing* D. *to* R. *of Rebecca, takes her* R. *arm.*)

REBECCA. (*Stumbles. Willard and Proctor support her.*) I have not had my breakfast. (*Willard on her* R., *Proctor on other, they go out.*)

PARRIS. Go to him, (*Drum roll off* U. R.) Goody Proctor! There is yet time! (*Parris runs out as though to hold back his fate.*) Proctor! Proctor! (*Elizabeth crosses to* U. S. *of window.*)

HALE. (*Crosses to entrance, turns.*) Woman, plead with him! (*Drum roll. Elizabeth avoids his eyes. Hale crosses to inside entrance.*) It is pride, it is vanity. Be his helper!—what profit him to bleed? Shall the dust praise him? (*Kneeling* U. S. *of Elizabeth.*) Shall the worms declare his truth? Go to him, take his shame away.

ELIZABETH. (*Firmly with bitter triumph.*) He have his goodness now. God forbid I take it from him. (*The drum roll heightens violently. Three seconds and then*)

THE CURTAIN FALLS

PROPERTY LIST

ACT I—SCENE 1

Walking stick for Rebecca
Heavy books for Hale

ACT I—SCENE 2

Gun (Proctor)
Small rag doll with needle in it (Mary)
2 warrants (Cheever)—1 destroyed each performance
Whip (Proctor)
Shawl (Elizabeth)
Towel on washstand
Basin with water in it on washstand
Dish of stew and spoon
Pewter mug with cider in it

ACT II—SCENE 1

Lantern (Proctor)

ACT II—SCENE 2

2 depositions (Proctor)
Petition signed by 91 people (Proctor)
Eyeglasses (Danforth)
Box with writing materials (Cheever)
Eyeglasses (Cheever)

ACT II—SCENE 3

2 lanterns (Willard)
Flask (Willard)
Dispatch case (Cheever)
Wooden writing box (Cheever)
Chains for Proctor's wrists. (May provide sound for Elizabeth's chains offstage in Act I—Scene 2)
Rags on benches to serve as bedclothes for Sarah and Tituba
Straw on benches
Eyeglasses for Cheever
Paper for Cheever to write on and Proctor to sign—destroyed each performance
Pen for Cheever